ISAIAH

THE PROPHET OF ZION

BRIAN SIMMONS

Isaiah

The Prophet of Zion

Brian Simmons

Isaiah: The Prophet of Zion

Isaiah by Brian Simmons
Published by Stairway Ministries
P.O. Box 26512
West Haven CT 06516
203-934-0880

ISBN 0-9753464-2-3
Printed in the United States of America

CONTENTS

INTRODUCTION

ISAIAH

THE PROPHET OF ZION

You are about to embark on a new journey, through the realm of mystery, to find the revelation and spirit of the prophet, Isaiah. He spoke for God. He saw the Lord seated on His throne. His lips burned with the purifying coal off the altar of holiness. He heard the song of seraphim. He challenged his nation and his words live on today.... Remarkable and rich, eloquent and majestic. This is the book of Isaiah!

The glory of God is its major theme. Isaiah's sweeping scope covers nearly 50 years of Israel's history and thousands of years of Israel's future. It is a book for today. It is yet to be 'cracked open' and enjoyed like precious fruit by this generation. God shines bright and His purpose is revealed through the prophecies of Isaiah!

The New Testament writers quote or refer to Isaiah over 200 times. Isaiah's message permeates the entire New Testament. He has at his command a vocabulary richer than any other prophet. The book of Isaiah needs to be studied as a literary work of art, viewed with eyes that appreciate its beauty. The imagery of Isaiah must be taken in as one would gaze on a masterpiece, drinking in the majesty and flowing with its movements.

Many Bible students have seen the correlation between Isaiah's 66 chapters and the 66 books of the Bible. The first 39 chapters of Isaiah paint a somewhat dark picture of the true condition of nations and the hearts of men. Likewise, the first 39 books of the Bible comprise the Old Testament, the Law and Prophets. Isaiah's last 27 chapters are filled with hope, mercy, compassion, and fulfillment of God's purposes on the earth. Likewise, the last 27 books of the Bible make up our New Testament, the story of our Lord Jesus Christ and His apostles who have released the Bride of Christ into the knowledge of her destiny.

The salvation of God is so clearly seen in Isaiah that many have called it the 'Gospel of Isaiah.' Jesus Christ is seen in the shadows of every prophecy in this book. Even though many see it as a book of judgment, grace shines forth. We must see Isaiah as the 'Book of Complete Deliverance.' God speaks through Isaiah and prophesies of a glorious people known as Zion who will arise on the earth to reveal the majesty of Yahweh to the nations. This 'Zion Company' will be a people of the Holy Place who flow in ministry out of the throne room.

There are three books of the Bible that are meant to be for the end of the age; three books for this generation that present a **Now** word for the church in America. They are being opened and illuminated by the Holy Spirit as never before in the history of the church.

Isaiah — The last days from an earthly perspective. (How we see God's judgments & the coming glory).

Revelation — The last days from a heavenly viewpoint (What the angels see).

Song of Songs — The glad Bridegroom. (What God feels about us even as He judges)

These three books combined give us a synopsis of what God is doing in heaven and on the earth, and how He feels about **You** while He is doing it. He is committed to removing everything that gets in the way of passionate love for the Bride. Be ready beloved, to see the King of the Nations in a way you have never seen Him before!

INTRODUCTION:

"And we have the word of the prophets made more certain,
And you will do well to pay attention to it,
As to a light shining in a dark place, Until the day dawns and the Morning Star rises in your hearts." — II Peter 1:19–20

I. THE PROPHETIC WRITINGS

The towering book of Isaiah stands at the head of the prophets. The Old Testament contains 16 named prophets who wrote books with their names attached. Four are known as Major Prophets simply because their books are greater length (Isaiah, Jeremiah, Ezekiel, Daniel). There are 12 known as Minor Prophets (Hosea, Joel, Amos, Obadiah, Jonah, Micah, Nahum, Habakkuk, Zephaniah, Haggai, Zechariah, and Malachi).[1]

The backgrounds and ministries of the prophets were all different. Isaiah seems to be a prophet who was a part of the royal line. There is no indication he attached himself to the Temple staff. Micah was a man of the countryside. Amos was a herdsman

Hosea was a farmer. Jeremiah belonged to the priestly family, but it was never stated that he served as a priest or was a member of the Temple staff. Ezekiel was to be a priest, but on his thirtieth year, he was visited by God in a whirlwind in a foreign land and called into the "watchman" ministry of prophetic intercession. Neither Zephaniah nor Haggai seem to have been priests or attached to the Temple. Habakkuk however, was likely a priest serving in Temple worship and carrying on prophetic ministry on the side. The same is true of Nahum, Joel, Zechariah and Malachi.

The prophets were unique and powerful in their ministry. Often, they were sent by God on dangerous missions to speak and preach to kings and enemies. They would be dispatched at the 11th hour to go and rescue a people headed for destruction. Sometimes their message was heard, but most of the time it was misunderstood and rejected. The prophets were burning men with burning hearts, who spent time with a burning God.

Isaiah speaks of himself and his children as prophetic signs: "Here am I, and the children the **Lord** has given me. We are signs and symbols in Israel from the **Lord** Almighty, who dwells on Mount Zion (8:18)." The prophets saw themselves as living messages, walking among the people as living, breathing words from God to the nations.

Each of the prophets spoke messages that were to endure beyond their days. They spoke not only to the people of their day, but they speak to us. The message of the prophets must be restored to the church if we are to move on toward the fullness of Christ. They are the equippers of the Old Testament that refused to leave people in the dark. They were men of hope and men of holiness. They expected God to keep His promises of restoration and revival.

History does not interpret prophecy. It is prophecy that interprets history. It is the speaking forth of the mind of Christ, shining light into a dark place. God's heart is revealed in the prophetic writings of the Scripture, pointing us all to the glory of Christ and the fullness of His increasing kingdom on this earth.

True prophecy will release power to unfold and implement divine strategy. This is precisely what happens through the revelation of Isaiah's writings. The key for understanding the entire Bible is Jesus Christ. We look for Him in the pages of the Word. When the prophets spoke, the life of Christ came forth by the Spirit of prophecy flowing through them. The Spirit of prophecy is the testimony of Jesus and is meant to convey the very thoughts of the mind of Christ. In a sense, the mind of Christ is the Spirit of prophecy.[2]

The prophetic writings include parables and allegories (i.e. Ezekiel 17). The prophets knew they were speaking profound and hard to understand truths (I Peter 1:10–12). They were quick to use symbols and types to teach the people God's point of view. God Himself used these pictures to teach His servants hidden truths (Jer.1:11–14, Ezekiel 1, Daniel 7, etc). **The prophets were poets, masters of the literary arts.** They themselves were deep wells from which God drew sacred water, to give us to drink.

It is important to note three things concerning the prophets:

1. **They saw the Lord.**
2. **They were sent on a mission by God.**
3. **They were set apart for God. The legitimacy of the prophet was his call.**

These are the three distinguishing elements of the prophetic voices raised up by the Lord to speak His Word to the people. Isaiah, Jeremiah, Ezekiel, and Daniel all speak of these things....

Isaiah — Cleansed with the coal of fire, he was sent after seeing the Lord.
Jeremiah — Chosen before his birth, God touched his mouth/ sent him to tear down and build up.

Ezekiel — Given a scroll to eat, he was sent to be a watchman and set apart with divine favor.

Daniel — Sent to Babylon he saw the ancient of Days and remained undefiled before the heathen.

The prophet is an inspired man. A mighty power works in him and speaks through him. The mysterious and "strong hand" of God would come upon them (Isa.8:11, Jer.15:17). The prophet of the Old Testament knew that it was God who placed the thoughts and words within him. The privilege of the prophet is to receive the burden, the word of the Lord as a wonderful gift from heaven. The responsibility of the prophet is to discharge that burden by speaking forth the revelations of God. The chief mission of every prophet was to carry God's word to His people ... whether they would receive it or not (Jer.3:10).

The prophet's task was not only to preach, but to be an intercessor for the people.[3] These prophet-intercessors impacted greatly their culture, changing the very worship of Yahweh. Through their prayers calamities were averted and judgments postponed. Great authority is given to God's prophets throughout the Bible.

II. ISAIAH — A BRIEF SKETCH OF HIS LIFE

Isaiah's name is a sign and a symbol from the Lord Almighty (8:18). Isaiah means, 'Yahweh is Salvation.' In that one name is compressed the entire contents of the book. Among the "woes" and thunderings of the Lord Almighty there is a message of God's salvation that cannot be hidden throughout Isaiah.

He was the son of Amoz (not Amos, the prophet). Amoz means 'to increase, to establish, to be strong or mighty.' The name Amoz is found in the Hebrew translation of Psalm 27:14, Deut.31:6,7, 23, Josh.1:6,7,9 and means — 'he shall strengthen' or 'good courage.'

Tradition has it that Isaiah was part of the royal family, nephew[4] to King Uzziah, which gave his ready access to the king. Isaiah was a royal prophet.

Isaiah was married. His wife is called, "the prophetess" (8:3), which indicates she also had a clear prophetic mantle upon her life. Together they had a high social standing in the land. They were a husband and wife prophetic team.

Isaiah had two sons, Shearjashub and Maher-shalal-hashbaz. The first name means, 'A remnant shall return' and the second means, 'quick to the plunder, swift to the spoil.'

God commissioned Isaiah into prophetic ministry (Isaiah 6). It is very likely that Isaiah knew the prophecies of Hosea, who ministered shortly before Isaiah's call.

His ministry falls within the range of four kings of Judah: Uzziah, Jotham, Ahaz, and Hezekiah. Some believe he even lived into the days of the reign of Manasseh. This would mean his ministry lasted almost 60 years.

Isaiah lived and ministered in Jerusalem (7:3, 22:15, 28:4, 37:2). He was known to have disciples who assisted him in his ministry (8:16). He wrote biographies of King Uzziah (II Chron.26:22), and King Hezekiah (II Chron.32:32). Isaiah was a literary genius, unequaled even by Homer, Shakespeare, or Milton. With brilliance of expression and versatility of imagery, he was a poet-prophet of the highest order.

The prophets often acted out the word of the Lord. Isaiah was not afraid of displaying prophetic deeds that described to the people what God was about to do. In Chapter 20 he went about for three years "stripped and barefoot," under the direction of God. What an example of humility, especially for one who was an aristocrat and polished writer/ speaker!

Isaiah was a patriot who loved his country. He uses the phrase, "my people" 26 times. He pleaded with Judah to return to God and warned her kings when they erred.

He was a man who hated sin and false religion. With great courage he boldly declared the Word of God, even when public opinion turned against him.

Hebrews 11:37 states that some men of faith "were sawed in two." Jewish historians believe this is what happened to Isaiah (See The Ascension of Isaiah).

III. MAJOR THEMES

The scope of Isaiah's prophecy is grand. It covers the highest themes of Scripture:

A. The holiness of God

Isaiah uses the word **Holy** more than all the other prophets combined.[5] The overthrow of all human greatness is prophesied by Isaiah as "the Lord alone will be exalted in that day (2:11,17)." The holiness of God is 'cubed' in chapter 6 to describe the magnitude of His glory. Isaiah is the prophet of holiness in the Old Testament.

B. The salvation of the Lord

This is the meaning of Isaiah's name, 'Yahweh Saves!' The unfolding of the salvation of God is seen throughout Isaiah's writings. Isaiah is the theologian of the Old Testament who teaches the people that God is their Redeemer and Savior. More than a poet, Isaiah is the Evangelist among the prophets.

C. The Messiah, Jesus Christ

The hope of the people of God is in the One who was to come, the Great Messiah, our Lord Jesus Christ. The word "Messiah" is taken from a root word meaning, 'dominion, officer, ruler, superintendent. The book of Isaiah gives us the most comprehensive life-story of the Messiah found in the all of the Old Testament. Isaiah is known as the 'Messianic Prophet' because he was captured with the revelation of the Messiah, the Branch of the Lord who would come and fully deliver the people of God until they became

His eternal dwelling place. Notice some of the details of Isaiah's vision of the Christ:

His Birth — (7:14)
His Authority — (9:11–12)
His Anointing — (11:1–3)
He is Judge — (2:4)
He Shines as a Great Light — (9:2)
He is the Intercessor — (53:12)
He is the Lawgiver — (42:4)
He is the Burden Bearer — (53:4)
He is the Sin Bearer — (53:6)
He is the Holy Liberator — (53:7)
He is silent before His accusers — (53:7)
He is beaten and spat upon — (50:6)
He is bruised for our iniquities — (53:5)
He died with the transgressors — (53:12)
He was buried with the rich — (53:9)
He was raised from the dead — (25:7–8)
He will reign eternally — (40:22–23, 66:1,22)

D. Zion, the city (people) of God

This is a prominent theme in the writings of Isaiah. Ancient commentaries have described Isaiah 28–35 as 'Zion's Book.' Zion is a metaphor for the people of God living in union with heaven. Israel is called Zion. The church is also designated as Zion. It is the ideal of God to bring His people into union with Himself in a realm called Zion. The King reigns in Zion. More than a mountain or a city, it is a relationship between the Lord and His people. The saga of the people of God and their city is the story line of the book of Isaiah.

E. The "holy seed"

The people of Zion are His "holy seed" (6:13), with the life of Immanuel coming forth in us. God and His people are one.

This divine union is prophesied and taught throughout Isaiah's prophecy. Jesus is the Branch and we are also branches that are joined to Him (4:2, 11:1, Jer. 23:5 John 15). He is the Anointed One and we are also anointed in Him. There is a corporate meaning to much of what is found in Isaiah, especially after chapter 53. The Lord wants to mingle Himself with His people and dwell with us in righteousness in the heavenly Jerusalem (33:20, Rev.21–22).

F. The judgment of the Lord

Warnings of judgment are found throughout Isaiah. As King and Creator, God has the authority and the right to judge the nations! None would escape if they did not repent. Yet, even in a time of judgment there is a God who will shield, protect, and mature His people.

[A Word About Justice]

Justice or judgment must be seen in a new way as we look through Isaiah's eyes. Every time God intervenes on the earth He is judging the kingdom of darkness that holds man in its grip. Judgment is one of God's ways of deliverance. Every healing is God's judgment on sickness. Salvation is God's judgment on Satan. Every time people in your city come to Christ, God is judging the strongholds of unbelief and darkness that keep others from the light of the gospel. Revival is an extension of God's judgment on evil. Unity is a judgment on division and strife, etc.

The Lord is about to change our perspective of judgment. We will begin to see justice as more than God striking out at rebellion. That is only a part of true justice. He wants a radiant people on the earth that love holiness more than compromise and hidden sin. Judgment will bring us to the place of no longer feeding our favorite demons by secret lifestyles. We will be a pure people who walk in the light of justice all our days. As the fear of God is established in our hearts, we will begin to join our voice with God's and declare His judgments on the earth.

Every prayer is actually a cry for justice to come to the earth. "And will not God bring about justice for his chosen ones, who cry out to him day and night? Will he keep putting them off? I tell you, he will see that they get justice, and quickly (Luke 18:7–8)." When God answers our day and night prayers (24 hours a day) it is called judgment. Prayer calls for subversion into the kingdom powers of the earth and release justice into the hearts of men. Prayer is a declaration of treason to the kingdom of darkness. Answered prayer is an act of judgment.

Many see the prophets as merely declaring harsh and angry words to a rebellious people. In fact, they are restorers and revivalists. Only a portion of their ministry was to deliver words of doom and gloom. The prophet's message of judgment always included restoration, a godly remnant, and the glory of God to be released. Judgment is not a mood but a method of God to raise up a holy seed on the earth that is free and disentangled from darkness.

IV. OUTLINE — THREE PORTRAITS OF CHRIST

A. The Anointed King (Chapters 1–39)

Book of Judgment — (Chapters 1–5)

Jehovah's Indictment (1)
Jehovah's Mountain (2)
Judah's Punishment (3)
The Branch Man (4)
Parable of the Vineyard (5)

Book of Commissioning — (Chapter 6)

Isaiah's Call (6)

Book of Immanuel — (Chapters 7–12)

The Coming Child (7)
Father & Sons — Signs & Wonders (8)

B. The Anointed Servant (Chapters 40–55)

The Servant's Task (Chapters 40–49)

The Message of Comfort (40)
The Message of Courage (41)
God's Perfect Servant: The Messiah (42)
God's Wayward Servant: His People (43)
The People's Choice: Idolatry (44)
God's Choice: Cyrus (45)
Calamity for Babylon (46–47)
Caution for Judah (48)

The Servant's Commitment (Chapters 49–52)[6]

The Servant & His Task of Restoration (49)
The Servant's Obedience & Israel's Sin (50)
The Servant & His Salvation (51)
The Exaltation of the Servant (52)

The Servant Completes His Task (Chapter 53)

The Suffering Servant (53)
The Servant Becomes Servants (Chapters 54–55)
The Servant's Song (54)
The Servant's Satisfaction (55)

C. The Anointed Conqueror (Chapters 56–66)

The Conqueror's Task (Chapters 56–59)

The Conqueror's Salvation to the Outcasts (56)
The Conqueror's Message to the Wicked (57)
The Conqueror's Message to the Righteous (58)
The Conqueror's Salvation (59)

The Conqueror's Commitment (Chapters 60–62)

Restoration of Judah (60–61)
Reunion with the Bridegroom (62)

The Conqueror Completes His Task (Chapters 63–65)

Remembering Mercy (63)
Repenting of Pride (64)
Reborn and Remade (65)

The Conqueror Becomes Conquerors (Chapters 66)

Rejoicing and Released! (66)

V. GLIMPSES OF CHRIST IN ISAIAH

Jesus Christ, the Owner of all — (1:3, Col.1)
Jesus Christ, the Rock — (2:10, 51:1, Matt.16:18)
Jesus Christ, the One Man — (4:1, Eph.4:13, 27)
Jesus Christ, the Beloved — (5:1, Matt.3:17)
Jesus Christ, the Lord on His throne — (6:1, Eph.1:18–23)
Jesus Christ, the King, Lord of Hosts — (6:5, Rev.19:16)
Jesus Christ, Immanuel — (7:14, Matt.1:21–23)
Jesus Christ, a Stone of stumbling — (8:14, I Pet.2:7–8)
Jesus & His Sons/ Isaiah & sons — (8:1–18, Heb.2:10–13)
Jesus Christ, the Root of Jesse — (11:1, 10, Matt.1:1)
Jesus Christ, the Highway — (11:16, John 14:6)
Jesus Christ, Strength & Salvation — (12:2,Eph.5:19–21)
Jesus Christ, the Holy One of Israel — (17:7, 44:24, Col.1)
Jesus Christ, the heavenly Eliakim — (22:20–22, Rev.3:7)
Jesus Christ, Refuge, Shelter, Shade — (25:4, Heb.4:14–16)
Jesus Christ, a Glorious Crown — (28:5, Heb.2:9–10)
Jesus Christ, a Precious Cornerstone — (28:16, I Pet.2:6)
Jesus Christ, the Righteous King — (32:1, Heb.1:8–9)
Jesus Christ, Sword from heaven — (34:5, Heb.4:12)
Jesus Christ, the Way of Holiness — (35:8, John 14:6)
Jesus Christ, the Glory of the Lord — (40:5, Heb.2:8–10)
Jesus Christ, God's Holy Arm — (40:10, Matt.28:18–20)
Jesus Christ, the Tender Shepherd — (40:11, John 10)
Jesus Christ, the Enthroned Creator — (40:22, 28, Rev.4–5)
Jesus Christ, the First and Last — (41:4, Rev.1:17, 22:13)

Jesus Christ, the Redeemer — (41:14, Gal.3:13–14)
Jesus Christ, the Servant — (42:1, 53:11, Phil.2:1–11)
Jesus Christ, a Light for the Gentiles — (42:6, Luke 2:32)
Jesus Christ, Mighty Man of War — (42:13, Eph.6:10–18)
Jesus Christ, the Heavenly Cyrus — (45:1, Luke 4:18)
Jesus Christ, the Polished Arrow — (49:2, Heb.4:12)
Jesus Christ, God's Banner — (49:22, John 12:32)
Jesus Christ, One with good news — (52:7, Rom.10:15)
Jesus Christ, Tender Shoot — (53:2, John15)
Jesus Christ, a Man of sorrows — (53:3, Heb.5:7)
Jesus Christ, Lamb led to slaughter — (53:7, Acts 8:32–33)
Jesus Christ, our Husband — (54:5, Eph.5:17–33)
Jesus Christ, Leader & Commander — (55:4, Eph.1:18–23)
Jesus Christ, Light & Glory — (60:1, John 8:12, Heb.2:9)
Jesus Christ, the Anointed One — (61:1–3, Luke 4:18)
Jesus Christ, Angel of His Presence — (63:9, John 1:14–18)
Jesus Christ, the Potter — (64:8, Col.1:15–18)
Jesus Christ, our River of Peace — (66:12, Eph.2:14)

---

[1] The New Testament also contains 4 gospels and 12 apostles to give us prophetic revelation.
[2] Revelation 19:10 & I Corinthians 2:14–16
[3] Genesis 20:7, 17
[4] Some believe he was the king's nephew or first cousin.
[5] Over 1/3 of all the references to God's holiness are found in Isaiah.
[6] Chapters 49–57 are often referred to as the Book of the Messiah, and Chapters 58–66 are described as the Book of Judah.

1

THE VISION

"THE VISION ... OF ISAIAH"

Isaiah is the prophet of Zion. He is not simply a teacher or preacher, but a seer for God's people. **Zion** is a supernatural people who live from a supernatural vision. Zion is not simply a spiritual place, it is a spiritual people. It is a realm of glory, a realm of vision.

You are about to enter a vision-zone of heaven descending upon earth. Come and study the vision of a man who saw the glory of God and now speaks with burning lips. True prophetic ministry flows from this "vision." It flows until it grows ... into a burden.

Breaking forth with a blast of newly released Spirit-wind,[1] Isaiah now speaks for God with fire-touched lips. His writings are described as **"The vision"** (Heb. 'chazon'). This word is a descriptive term for the entire supernatural revelation given by God to Isaiah. It is the supernatural reality of Yahweh breaking into the reality of this world.

The heading of the book of Isaiah is a challenge to see this enormous collection of prophecies, (the longest in the Bible), as ***The Vision***. It is not simply teaching or an historical record — it is the over arching vision of the heart of God revealed to His seer-prophet.

This *vision* spans the plan of the ages. It becomes a collective overview of all that God has planned. In takes us beyond the days of Isaiah, even beyond our own times, bringing us into the council chambers of eternity, revealing the unfolding plan of an all-wise God. The vision truly did not belong to Isaiah, but to the LORD.

ISAIAH'S INSPIRATION — 1:1

"The vision concerning Judah and Jerusalem that Isaiah son of Amoz saw during the reigns of Uzziah, Jotham, Ahaz and Hezekiah, kings of Judah." Isaiah's words go beyond the immediate historical context and speak into our immediate internal context. The scope of this book touches every nation on the earth today. The prophecies of Isaiah are addressed not only to the citizens of the 8th century B.C. but also to the inhabitants of the whole earth — *"with all of us who are alive here today"* (Deut.5:3).

With panoramic insight, Isaiah preaches about the virgin birth of Christ and the virgin Bride of Christ. We read prophecies of the new thing God delights in doing and the New Jerusalem God delights to dwell in. We see Christ Jesus as the Man of Sorrows and the Conquering King. Isaiah's burning message is not only for the future, it is for **Now**.

Even the names mentioned in verse one have something to teach us. **Amoz** means, 'to be made strong or courageous.' **Judah** means, 'praise.' Isaiah prophesied during the reign of **Uzziah** ('the power of Yahweh' or 'mighty is Yahweh'), **Jotham** ('the one Yahweh makes perfect' or 'Yahweh is upright'), **Ahaz** ('possessor' or 'to lay hold of'), and **Hezekiah** ('strengthened by Yahweh' or 'the one Yahweh makes firm').

Here is what the names of verse 1 teach us:

We can see that prophetic vision from a *'courageous'* prophet imparts *'the power of Yahweh,'* which releases those whom *'Yahweh makes perfect'* to maturity. They will be *'possessors'* and those who 'lay hold of' heaven's promises until they are *'strengthened by Yahweh'* and *'made firm'* in all their ways! All of will take place in the land of *'praise'*!

Isaiah's book is a living picture that speaks to living men today, as personally and practically as it did when it was first spoken. This first chapter is considered by many as one of the most powerful human speeches given in history. Isaiah lines up true witnesses that will prove to Israel that she has abandoned God. One after another witnesses will take the stand to present their case.

Every time God's people looked into the sky, or down to the earth (v.1–2) — every time they saw the ox or donkey returning to their owners (v.3), every time they saw a leper or bruised individual (v.4–6), and every time their crops were harvested (7–9) they were seeing another witness to their sin. It is the duty of the prophet to warn the people of their evil.

THE COURT CONVENED — 1:2

"Hear, O heavens! Listen, O earth! For the *LORD* has spoken: "I reared children and brought them up, but they have rebelled against me."

The time has come to listen to God. Earth must agree with heaven,[2] for the Lord has spoken. Heaven and earth must obey the voice of the Lord. They are the *two witnesses* God uses against His people (Deut.19:15). These searching words have an implicit message to us: Will we listen and obey. The heavens will obey. The earth will obey. The winds and waves will obey — but will we?

The voice of the Lord breaks through. The God who raises up mature sons and daughters has something to teach us. The words used for **"reared"** and **"brought them up"** are two Hebrew synonyms that could be translated *'exalt, advance, set on high, mature, increase, magnify, promote, raise up, and cause to grow.'* This is what God will do for His children.[3]

Here is the key left under the doormat to the book of Isaiah. It is a study of God's ways of exalting His people, His Bride, making them into mature children who will increase His kingdom and implement His government.

With great tenderness and patience God has redeemed (reared) and nurtured His people. He "brought them up" out of Egypt, making Israel a great nation upon the earth (Deut.4:32–34, II Sam.7:23). He has also made His church a holy nation of priests to serve Him (I Pet.2:9). Yet, Isaiah makes it clear: "They have rebelled[4] against Me!" We are all juvenile delinquents.

The sin of ingratitude is what ultimately leads to rebellion. Isaiah records God's words about those who do not grow intimate and understanding of who He really is. The apostle Paul takes us down this same road (Romans 1:21–31). Paul taught the church that rebellion begins with an unthankful heart that will not acknowledge the care and mercies of God.

The book of Isaiah (and the book of Romans) opens with the drama of a courtroom and the drop of the opening gavel. God assembles His heavenly courtroom to verify the justice of what is about to come to the earth. The entire universe is called as a witness to the divine indictment[5] against His people. There is a Great Judge whose Name is Mighty, there are reliable witnesses (heaven and earth), a prosecuting attorney (the prophet Isaiah) and a defendant (the people of God).

THE MASTER AND THE MANGER — 1:3

"The ox knows his master, the donkey his owner's manger, but Israel does not know, my people do not understand."

The two animals that we consider the most stupid and stubborn are used to describe God's rebellious people. You may have heard the expression, 'Dumb as an ox,' or 'Stubborn as a mule (donkey).' When we do not understand all that God has done for us and do not consider Him, we are worse than a donkey or an ox.

At least the ox knows his master; God's people seem to be unaware of the incredible opportunity before us to be intimate with the God of heaven. At least the donkey knows where his master will feed him, while God's people do not understand where we can be fed and strengthened by the Word and by the Spirit. It is time to know the Master and His manger.

How many times do we not even show the intelligence or responsiveness of an ox or donkey? Those that God has faithfully nourished do not even understand Him or know His purpose for them. The ox and the mule have learned to submit to their master and be fed and cared for. They are both loyal and attached to their master. They know the hand that feeds them and recognize the one who is kind to them.

How much does our Master long to take us to the manger[6] (the place of feeding, i.e. local church) and feed us from His hand (5-fold ministry)! It is time to know and understand the "vision" of the Lord and submit to His perfect care. As privileged sons and daughters, we must know our Father intimately and be meek as He leads us to His manger. How can we ignore our Father?

THE INDICTMENT — 1:4

"Ah, sinful nation, a people loaded with guilt, a brood of evildoers, children given to corruption! They have forsaken the Lord; they have spurned the Holy One of Israel and turned their backs on him."

Can you imagine a prophet of God going to the White House or to Congress, dressed in camel hair, prophesying these words to America? It begins with the word "Ah," or 'Alas!' The grief of God cannot be contained. With the heavens looking down, the Creator lays before His people a 7-fold indictment: **"Ah, sinful nation."** No longer holy or set apart, sin had become linked to their identity. They were guilt-burdened, for sin will always leave **"a people loaded with guilt."** We ought to be a people loaded with holiness and passion to be fully His!

The earth agrees with the weeping God as He calls His own people, **"a brood[7] of evildoers."** As God's very own, they have become **"children given to corruption,"** or literally, 'children who destroy and lay waste what is right.'

The rest of the verse gives three more causes for the sorry state of God's people. **"They have forsaken the Lord."** What could be a greater evil than to forsake the Father who reared you? We have a personal relationship with our Covenant God, why would anyone turn his or her back on **"the Holy One of Israel?"** We are called to be holy but so often turn backwards.

The word **"spurned"** is actually 'despised, provoked, condemned, blasphemed.' This is even more serious when it is the Holy One of Israel[8] that is being dishonored. If all of this is true, and it is, then the moral and spiritual condition of God's people was extremely desperate. This is a timeless word from God describing those who **"turned their backs on Him."**

[Note: Isaiah uses four terms for the people of God: nation, people, seed, and sons. We find here seven descriptions of those who have forsaken the Lord. They are sinful, loaded with guilt, evildoers, given to corruption, forsaking the Lord, despising the Holy One, and turning their backs on Him.]

THE INDICTMENT — 1:5–6

"Why should you be beaten anymore? Why do you persist in rebellion? Your whole head is injured, your whole heart afflicted. From the sole of your foot to the top of your head there is no soundness — only wounds and welts and open sores, not cleansed or bandaged or soothed with oil."

This is more the lament of a Father than the indictment of a Judge. The breaking heart of God is unveiled to His disobedient and prodigal people. He is the only One who could truly say to His erring children, 'This hurts Me more than it does you.' Can you hear the deep tone of pitying wonder as God pleads with us, **"Why should you be beaten anymore?"** The truth is, we gain nothing by putting distance between God and us except being beaten by our sins, our guilt, and our conscience.

The word for "beaten" is the word used in Exodus for the sending of plagues upon Egypt. We are judged by God and open ourselves to the plagues of punishment if we turn away.

Again, God asks why? His question is meant to burn in our heart until we repent: **"Why do you persist in rebellion?"** This is the logic of God. He pleads in mercy to question our ways until our conscience comes alive again. Long before He sends judgment, God sends conviction to pry its way into our hearts.

The injured **"head"** speaks of at least two things: the leadership of the nation and the thoughts that have excluded God. With the gaze of a physician, God sees the true illness of His people. They have a fatal wound and a fatal disease, which if it is not treated, will bring them to destruction. They have been beaten and wounded severely and must seek a cure.

The feeble and afflicted **"heart"** speaks of their devotion and desire after God. The whole heart is afflicted when we have no passion to pursue the Father God who raised us up on high to sit with Him (Eph.2:6). From head to toe the people are sick and weak ... all because of drawing away from the divine presence.

"Wound, welts, and open[9] **sores"** is a horrifying description of how we appear to the Holy One of Israel when we refuse to walk in His ways. The bruises and sores of walking in pride always leave us as one of the walking wounded. Our heart-wounds result from turning from God, not merely our circumstances or caused by other people.

"From the sole of your foot (our walk) **to the top of your head** (our thought life) **there is no soundness...."** Yet with God, we could come at any time and have our wounds **"cleansed,"** our welts **"bandaged,"** and our sores **"soothed with oil"** if we would only repent (Luke 4:18). This is a beautiful description of God's longings to heal us and make us complete in Him.

The cleansing of His endless love will heal any injury. The bandages of beauty will transform our bruises. The soothing oil of the Spirit can release healing to the deepest of sores.[10] The bleeding of our heart stops the moment we submit to God and receive His healing. It may not be painless, but it will be thorough. He is ever and always Jehovah-Rapha, the Lord our Healer.

[Note: Jesus was wounded for our transgressions and was beaten so badly that He was bruised from head to foot. His open sores bring us life and healing. Jesus took the very punishment described here in Isaiah Chapter One ... and He took it all for ***You****!]*

[1] All of God's words are inspired or 'God-breathed.' The term 'Spirit-wind' is the way I have chosen to describe the inspiration of prophetic speech coming from God to earth through His prophets.

[2] Many times in the Old Testament the heavens and earth are summoned as witnesses to an oath, or as witnesses for the prosecution when the Lord charges His people (Deut.4:26, Ps.50:4, Jer.2:12).

[3] In the book of Isaiah, God's love toward Israel is displayed in a three-fold way. He is Father (1:2–3, 63:16, 64:8), as a nursing Mother (66:13), and as a Husband (54:5). God was Israel's Father, Mother, and Husband.

[4] The Hebrew word indicates the breaking of a contract — the covenant Israel entered into with Yahweh was broken by their idolatry and unbelief.

[5] Throughout this chapter we see God speaking to the conscience of His people. Prophetic ministry must not be pointed to the emotions or to the mind, but to the conscience.

[6] Isn't it interesting that Jesus was laid in the donkey's manger at His birth? The "owners manger" is the birth of our Lord Jesus Christ, who has come to feed us His Living Bread.

[7] This is the word "seed" that is used in Genesis 3:15–16 for the "seed" of the woman and the "seed" of the serpent. The book of Isaiah is the story of those two seeds and the ultimate release and maturity of the Divine Seed coming forth in God's overcoming people (i.e. Immanuel, the Branch-Man, the Servant, etc.) See also Matthew 3:7–10.

[8] This is one of Isaiah's favorite terms for God, used 25 times.

[9] This is the word for 'putrefying' or 'dripping' sores.

[10] As the Good Samaritan, Jesus will do this for any of His injured ones (Luke 10:34).

2

SURVIVORS

"HEAR THE WORD OF THE LORD...."

True survivors are on their way. These survivors know the Lord and have walked through the fires of the cross and self-judgment required by heaven. Isaiah sees a remnant of survivors who will appear. Forsaking the Lord had left the land desolated and overthrown by strangers. The Lord lifts His hands of protection off of His people. They have become like a city under siege by foreigners (i.e. terrorists) much stronger than they.

God longed to have the cities of Israel (and our cities) burn with passion and devotion to God; instead the cities burned with the fires of judgment Sin had brought a curse to the land. The fields that were meant to provide food were stripped of their produce in the very sight of the ones who cultivated the fields.

"Your country is desolate, your cities burned with fire; your fields are being stripped by foreigners right before you, laid waste as when overthrown by strangers. The Daughter of Zion is left like a shelter in a vineyard, like a hut in a field of melons, like a city under siege."

God's judgment now takes the form of military powers coming against them. Wherever they turn there is sickness and devastation. All of this is meant to awaken the heart to righteousness and bring them to repentance. Yet in the midst of devastation God calls His people the "Daughter of Zion." The people of God are seen as God's daughter, born out of the Holy Place.

In the divine presence (Mt. Zion) God has given birth to His people. They are meant to be His dwelling place, instead they have become like a flimsy shelter or hut. The work of God as seen in the book of Isaiah is to restore this "hut" to the place of the Divine Shelter or Dwelling Place (read Isaiah 66). Even the besieged city will one day become the New Jerusalem, where God and man mingle as one.

"Unless the *LORD* Almighty had left us some survivors, we would have become like Sodom, we would have been like Gomorrah."[11]

The Lord Almighty ('Lord of Armies') will make sure there are some survivors (Ps.124). He will have a remnant, a band of "survivors" (4:2–3). Nothing will hinder the majestic God from fulfilling His plan. The failure of humanity cannot prevent the Lord of Armies from succeeding, even if He must start over (6:11–13).

With the motive of convicting the heart, God compares His people to Sodom and Gomorrah. Both the people of God and the people of Sodom were guilty. But with His redeemed, mercy will triumph and God will win in the end. If mercy had not stood up, the sword of judgment would have finished its strange work until the nation would be destroyed. But mercy won, it triumphed over judgment. God will leave survivors, refugees in the land. A *"holy seed"* (6:13) will spring up.

The promise of restoration is clear. All of our sin and all of our guilt will be as nothing before the Redeemer who will save completely those who come to God through Him (Heb.7:25, Isa.61:4). This theology of God preserving a remnant meant so much to Isaiah that he named one of His sons, Shear-jashub, 'a remnant will return' (7:3).

MEANINGLESS OFFERINGS — 1:10–11

"Hear the word of the *LORD*, you rulers of Sodom; listen to the law of our God, you people of Gomorrah! "The multitude of your sacrifices — what are they to me?" says the *LORD*. "I have more than enough of burnt offerings, of rams and the fat of fattened animals; I have no pleasure in the blood of bulls and lambs and goats."

Now the divine voice summons the *people* to listen, not just the heavens. The rulers and the people are walking in the same spirit of rebellion and refusal to obey the Lord as the people of Sodom and Gomorrah. God addresses them as **"the rulers of Sodom,"** and **"the people of Gomorrah."**

God doesn't need another sacrifice. Sin cannot be covered by the **"multitude"** of offerings and sacrifices, only by a repentant heart that trusts in mercy. Great and numerous sacrifices do not impress God. False dedication cannot move Him. He is moved by tears and heart-searching repentance, not by the blood of animals (false dedication). Our carnal, half-hearted devotion is nothing more than the fat of fattened animals (stuffed with the Word but not living it out).

God cannot be bought. He looks at the heart and requires offerings given in holiness and truth. The sacrifice of a fattened animal is an outward picture of what God wants to do inside of us.

He wants to kill that fleshly part of us that is only stuffed with the letter of the Word. That part of us offends Him and hinders His love from conquering out hearts. The death of self with its agenda is what He requires.

There is a pleasure we can bring to God every time we go low in humility and own up to our own wickedness. The sacrifice and blood of animals will fail to touch the heart of God but your crying will. This is what 'the Lord keeps saying.'[12]

[Note: There is a sacrifice revealed that does indeed bring pleasure to the Lord and removes our sin. It is the pleasing sacrifice of Jesus Christ on Calvary. The Lord takes pleasure every time He looks at the Cross.]

MEANINGLESS OFFERINGS — 1:12–14

"When you come to appear before me, who has asked this of you, this trampling of my courts? Stop bringing meaningless[13] offerings! Your incense is detestable to me. New Moons, Sabbaths and convocations — I cannot bear your evil assemblies. Your New Moon festivals and your appointed feasts my soul hates.[14] They have become a burden to me; I am weary of bearing them."

Even intercession (incense) can be detestable to God. We don't need another prayer meeting if we are not going to pray with broken hearts. God is asking for a refund and canceling His registration to our conferences! To God, they are only New Moon festivals, celebrating the new phase or new ideas or new strategies the clever church has come up with! He calls them, "your appointed feasts," not His.

All of this is a "burden" to God. Can you see His burden? To clean our hearts and make us a living sacrifice where the altar of prayer is continually burning up the unclean things inside of us!

Notice the words of Amos: *"I hate, I despise your religious feasts; I cannot stand your assemblies. Even though you bring me burnt offerings and grain offerings, I will not accept them. Though you bring choice fellowship offerings, I will have no regard for them. Away with the noise of your songs! I will not listen to the music of your harps. Let justice roll on like a river, righteousness like a never-failing stream!"* — Amos 5:21–24

Can you imagine God hiding His eyes from our prayer meetings? Even though we pray many prayers God hides His eyes from an unrepentant people (Ps.68:18). The Lord refuses to listen if we have not been washed from our sins. Intercession cannot hide our sin or cover our wickedness.

MAKE YOURSELVES CLEAN — 1:15–17

"When you spread out your hands in prayer, I will hide my eyes from you; even if you offer many prayers, I will not listen. Your hands are full of blood; wash and make yourselves clean. Take your evil deeds out of my sight! Stop doing wrong, learn to do right! Seek justice, encourage the oppressed. Defend the cause of the fatherless, plead the case of the widow."

The Lord's stinging words are these: '**Wash!** Make yourselves clean. Take evil deeds away from His eyes, stop doing ... etc. Hide nothing, then come and we'll talk.' This is the very cry of John the Baptist: "Produce fruit in keeping with repentance." — Matt 3:8.

Learning to do right involves ministry to the poor and downtrodden. Our godliness must take the form of justice and mercy or it is a sham and a pretense. The Father is looking for those who will encourage, not exploit the oppressed. He is looking for those who will defend the fatherless and widow, not ignore them. This was the clear practice of the early church — taking care of the worthy widows (I Tim.5). The 9 requirements of God from these verses correspond to the 9 fruits of the Spirit (Gal.5:22–23):

Wash!
Make yourselves clean!
Take away evil!
Stop doing wrong!
Learn to do right!
Seek justice!
Encourage the oppressed!
Defend the fatherless!
Plead for the widow!

LET US REASON TOGETHER — 1:18–20

"Come now, let us reason[15] together," says the *LORD*. "Though your sins are like scarlet,[16] they shall be as white as snow; though they are red as crimson, they shall be like wool."

Come *now* — **after** you have dealt with the issues of hypocrisy and superficial spirituality. This is not God asking man to come and debate Him over our guilt or innocence. Rather, God is saying, 'Let's get the matter settled. We cannot bargain for our salvation, but we can plead mercy when we realize our guilt. God's terms of surrender are absolute. We must come to Him in humility, repentance, and sincerity.

Things are not right between our nation and our God. It used to be we pointed our fingers of condemnation at those televangelists who were hypocrites. But before this decade is over, there will be holy men and women on TV who will point their fingers at you and tell you the party is over and it is time to repent.

God is very reasonable … but His reasoning is not like ours. Human reasoning is if your sins are as scarlet you must leave and pay the price of rebellion. God has an outrageous mercy. He is unreasonably kind. Until you see the scarlet stain of your sin you will not receive the mercy He extends.

The word for "crimson" is *'tola'* or **Worm**. All of our sins have made us like a worm. Even Jesus Himself used this expression to describe Himself as He took our sins upon Himself at the cross (Psalm 22:6). Crimson dye was made by crushing the crimson grub worm. This is what sin does to us all.

"Snow" and **"wool"** are both naturally white. The Lord will not only deal with our outward sins, but He has the power and will to cleanse our nature, changing us from the inside out.

"If you are willing and obedient, you will eat the best from the land; but if you resist[17] and rebel, you will be devoured by the sword. For the mouth of the *LORD* has spoken."

Willing and obedient, if you resist and rebel, you will be eaten. Either you will eat the best or you will be eaten by the worst. You will be devoured by the sword. The mouth of Yahweh has spoken this.

The best of the land is your inheritance — what you are meant to receive. It will be just what you need. More than you asked for, different than what you expected but just what will make you happy. This is the land of grace that the meek inherit. The best of the land is the fruits of the life of Jesus (Gal.5:22 — the harvest of the Spirit). The devouring sword is the flashing sword of the Word, exposing and piercing to the innermost part of our being (Heb.4:12).

THE FAITHFUL CITY — 1:21–25

"See how the faithful city has become a harlot! She once was full of justice; righteousness used to dwell in her — but now murderers! Your silver has become dross, your choice wine is diluted with water. Your rulers[18] are rebels, companions of thieves; they all love bribes and chase after gifts. They do not defend the cause of the fatherless; the widow's case does not come before them."

The people of God are called His Faithful City. The ultimate purpose of the Lord is to make us into the New Jerusalem Bride that comes out of heaven ready and faithful. God speaks through Isaiah and looks back with tender remembrance to the time His people were **"full of justice: righteousness used to dwell in her** (them)." But His people have committed spiritual adultery and are called **"a harlot!"** The glory has vanished. Now murder is within the walls of the city.

What was silver (redemption) has now become dross. The choice wine (gifts of the Spirit, truths of Pentecost) have become watered down and unintelligible. The gifts of God had been diluted by fleshly lives that did not measure up to the standard of holiness, they simply used their gift! Choice wine of the Spirit ruined by the works of the flesh.

Those in authority have become self-centered racketeers who love bribes (merchandising the anointing) but are no help to the poor and needy. This harlot city (church) is a picture of the last day's people who profess Christ but have no practical godliness to confirm it.

But God will have a faithful city. It will be the Bride of His Son, the New Jerusalem. It will come down out of heaven as a Bride adorned for her husband. This Bridal City will be the ultimate and eternal dwelling place where God and man mingle as one.... Then it will be understood the truth of Immanuel — God with us.

"Therefore the LORD, the *LORD* Almighty, the Mighty One of Israel, declares: Ah, I will get relief from my foes and avenge myself on my enemies. I will turn my hand against you; I will thoroughly purge away your dross and remove all your impurities."

Notice the names of God placed together: The Lord, the **Lord** Almighty, the Mighty One of Israel. There should be no doubt about what God is about to declare. The time of cleansing has come. The Lord has overheard all the cries of injustice and violation that have come from the lips of the oppressed and abused.

The enemies that live in you will be judged by a holy God. He promises to turn His hand against our favorite sins, those that are culturally accepted, and completely overturn our lives. Silver that has become dross has totally degenerated. It looks hopeless and impossible for God to restore righteousness and brilliant holiness to the church again. Yet, He will have a people who are clean, who shine bright for they are purged from impurity.

RETURN OF THE JUDGES — 1:26–28

"I will restore your judges as in days of old, your counselors as at the beginning. Afterward you will be called the City of Righteousness, the Faithful City."

The Lord promises to restore the 'breaker anointing.' These judges are deliverers, sent-ones with the power and righteousness of God flowing through them. They will be like Joseph, like Daniel, like Samson, like Elijah, and like John the Baptist. They will come with hearts on fire and lips anointed to burn up the dross within the church. They will be everything we have prayed for and everything we want to run from at the same time — Deliverers!

> *"Deliverers will go up on Mount Zion to govern the mountains of Esau. And the kingdom will be the **LORD's**."* — Obadiah 21

We need both the ministry of judges (apostolic) and the ministry of counselors (prophetic). The counselors will arise with extraordinary gifts from God to set people free. Their words of wisdom will pinpoint the exact area in the human spirit where sin has lodged and remained hidden.

The day will come when both the apostolic and prophetic will flow together with such grace and power that God's people will come swiftly into maturity and anointing for ministry.

Apostolic judges and prophetic counselors are on their way! Just like in days of old (Book of Acts). They are sent to challenge the status quo and make us consider our ways. The result of their needed ministry is that God's people will become the Faithful City and restored to be the City (Church) of righteousness. This is Isaiah's glimpse of the New Jerusalem, the Bridal City coming to the earth. It will be a "City of Righteousness" for God will dwell with His people.

"Zion will be redeemed with justice, her penitent ones with righteousness. But rebels and sinners will both be broken, and those who forsake the *Lord* will perish."

Zion will arise. Zion is God's term for His intimate Bride. Zion is a people not just a place. Justice will be the tool of restoration in God's hand as He redeems us from our evil. Those who return to Him bowing low in repentance will be redeemed and rescued with righteousness. But those who refuse to repent are described as **"rebels and sinners"** who will one day be broken and perish forever.

AN OAK WITH FADING LEAVES — 1:29–31

"You will be ashamed because of the sacred oaks[19] in which you have delighted; you will be disgraced because of the gardens that you have chosen. You will be like an oak with fading leaves, like a garden without water. The mighty man will become tinder and his work a spark; both will burn together, with no one to quench the fire."

Oaks and gardens are clearly used here for idol worship. The truth about idolatry is this: You become like what you worship. Since they worshipped their gods among the sacred oaks, they will be like an oak with fading leaves.

Since they have chosen the trees and gardens of human wisdom (counterfeit 'Edens'), they will become a waterless, barren garden. Fading leaves and gardens without water … so near their end. Their confidence becomes their destruction. In all their worship their conscience has gone asleep and they are drenched in wickedness. The works of mighty man (secular humanism) will become fuel for judgment fires, with no one who will come to quench those flames.

It is as though they have become flammable material and are playing with fire! This chapter is like a parable of the human conscience. In the end, all mankind will be forced to reason with God and enter into this eternal courtroom, ready or not.

This chapter drags us all before the austerity and holiness of God Himself. We are left undone, trembling, with no other hope than **Mercy**. The One we have offended is a Friend and a Father, if we will only turn in repentance and be covered in crimson blood. Conscience speaking within is nothing less than a Father's voice....

---

[11] This is the first verse from Isaiah that is quoted in the New Testament (Rom.9:29).

[12] "Says the Lord," is more accurately translated, 'The Lord keeps saying.'

[13] "Meaningless offerings" is literally, 'gifts of nothing.'

[14] Or, 'I hate with all My heart.'

[15] Some have translated this: 'Come now, let us bring our reasoning to an end.' This is God's call to end human reasoning and settle every issue before Him.

[16] The word for "scarlet" is taken from a root word meaning 'double, or repeated.' Even habitual sin can be cleansed if we repent.

[17] "Resist and rebel" — subtle resistance leads to blatant rebellion.

[18] This is a pun in Hebrew: 'Your rulers are unruly' or, 'Your princes are unprincipled.'

[19] The Hebrew word for "sacred oaks" (also called 'terebinth') rhymes with the Hebrew word for false gods. It is a play on words that is common to the prophets. The Baal cult worshipped at the groves of sacred oaks.

3

The Mountain

"The Mountain of the Lord's Temple will be established as chief among the mountains"

Isaiah pleads in Chapter 1, but in Chapter 2, he prophesies. The glory of God is coming to the earth, but it will be mingled with judgment. It will be a glorious display of His judgment. If our hearts are not right we will be offended with what God allows to come to our land. The Loving Bridegroom is also our Righteous Judge.

The vision of Isaiah is an outlook. It is a clear insight into the future purposes of God. Isaiah sees a day of great blessing when everything points to the **"mountain of the Lord's Temple,"** God's dwelling place with man. Mountains in the Scriptures are metaphors for governments and kingdoms. They are like hills and mountains on the landscape of history. They are raised up and brought down by the will of God. Some governments exist for centuries and some but for a generation. Yet there will be a mountain that will excel all other mountains. It will be the place where God's authority and government is established on earth.

Much of God's work has been accomplished on mountains. Mt. Sinai was where the word of the Lord thundered forth. Mt. Moriah was the place where Abraham was to sacrifice his son, Isaac. Mt. Calvary was the place where Jesus was crucified between two thieves to provide salvation for all.

Raised up to the place of honor, the Mountain of the Lord, God's dwelling place will eclipse all other kingdoms and earthly temples. It will be the chief of mountains, the highest of all hills. The secular world sees Christ's kingdom as irrelevant and powerless. But one day the kingdoms of the earth will be leveled and the King's Mountain will be high and exalted. With no rival, Jesus will sit enthroned. This optimistic outlook must be seen as the backdrop for all that Isaiah preaches. The prophet sings Zion's hymn of hope.

"The last days" speak of the days in which we are living. The Hebrew word for Chronicles is literally, 'the days.' It is the human history of Israel recorded within the pages of the Chronicles. The last days would speak of the final days of human history. In Hebrews 1:1–2 we learn that we are now living in the "last days." These last days began with Christ's appearing in Galilee and will culminate with Christ appearing in His Church. Peter quoted Joel in Acts 2 and applied them to what happened on Pentecost in the upper room — *"In the last days."* If the last days began 2,000 years ago, how much closer are we to the end of time today!

"Dear children, this is the last hour." — I John 2:18

The supremacy of this mountain-kingdom will release a worldwide revival. **"All nations will stream"**[20] to the mountain of the Lord to worship and bow before the holiness of earth's King. Revelation knowledge will cover the globe as paths of heaven touch the earth (Micah 4:1–4). Every nation will be given the invitation to ascend the Hill of the Lord and go up to worship Jesus Christ.

This is the New Jerusalem coming down out of heaven as a Bride adorned for her Bridegroom. The peoples of the earth will surrender spontaneously to the Divine truth of God dwelling with man. Listen to the words of John the apostle as he speaks Isaiah's language:

> *"Then I saw a new heaven and a new earth, for the first heaven and the first earth had passed away, and there was no longer any sea. I saw the Holy City, the New Jerusalem, coming down out of heaven from God, prepared as a bride beautifully dressed for her husband. And I heard a loud voice from the throne saying, "Now the dwelling of God is with men, and he will live with them. They will be his people, and God himself will be with them and be their God. "Come, I will show you the bride, the wife of the Lamb." And he carried me away in the Spirit to a mountain great and high, and showed me the Holy City, Jerusalem, coming down out of heaven from God. It shone with the glory of God, and its brilliance was like that of a very precious jewel, like a jasper, clear as crystal."*
> — Revelation 21:1–3, 9–12

The Temple will rise. It will be lifted up. It will mature and come forth. Even Paul the apostle taught this to the church at Ephesus: *"In Him* ***[Christ]*** *the whole building is joined together and rises to become a holy temple in the LORD. And in him you too are being built together to become a dwelling in which God lives by his Spirit (Eph.2:21–22)."* This rising Temple will one day dominate the earth as Church of Christ gives way to the City of God.

ZION

The mountain of the Lord's Temple is Mt. Zion, the place where God is enthroned. Zion was originally a Canaanite stronghold that was conquered by David (II Sam.5:7). Later, Zion began to signify the greater Temple area. Today, Zion is a synonym of the people of God, the Dwelling Place of His Spirit (Heb.12:22–24). God calls it, "My holy hill." Notice what the Scriptures say about Zion:

Zion in the Scriptures is where the Throne of God is eternally established (Ps.2:6, 87:5). It is the Dwelling Place of God, where He receives glory and praise (Ps.9:11, 74:2, 76:2).

Mt. Zion is the source of a continual salvation and revival manifestations of increasing fullness (Ps.14:7, 53:6, Isa.46:13, 59:20, Joel 2:32). It is the joy of the whole earth, experienced already by many, anticipated by others (Ps.48:2).

Zion is the source of strength and safety for the people of God in their day of trouble (Ps.20:2, 48:12). We see from **Zion** why God judges the earth, for in **Zion**, we come to know a true perspective of His righteousness (Ps.48:11, 97:8, Isa.33:5).

The perfection of beauty is in **Mt. Zion**, where the light of God shines forth (Ps.50:2). Perfected praise rises to the Lord in this place of perfect rest (Ps.65:1). The Mountain of Zion is where the Lord is known in His greatness (Ps.99:2, Isa.12:4–6). It is the hope of all the afflicted (Ps.102:16–22, Isa.14:32, 51:11).

Zion is where God reigns in the now! It is the realm from which His scepter of strength is stretched forth (Ps.110:2, Isa.14:23). Zion is **Known**, it is not traced with a boundary. Zion is **Experienced**. It is the Most Holy Place with all of its revelation and glory. Zion is becoming a present reality (Heb.12:22–24). Zion will become a people, the people of God! The **Overcomers** in the book of Revelation is the Zion Company, Joel's Army, the Ascending Angels on the Jesus Stairway, the Zadok Priesthood, a company of full grown sons, the Manchild, who has come to the measure of the fullness of the stature of Christ!

Zion is the realm where the Word of the Lord flows (Isaiah 2:1–3). Yahweh's laws stream forth into the hearts of men when we walk in Zion's ways.

The church is a city set on a hill, on a mountain (Mt. Zion) and cannot be hidden. The light of Zion is the light of Christ within the church!

Upon this Hill of Holiness, Mt. Zion, Jesus will Reign as King. Nothing can stop Him, no alliance can stop Him, no political party or United Nations will prevent Jehovah's King from raising His iron scepter.... There is nothing to fear. The appointed King is reigning in His church on Mt. Zion.

A supernatural magnetism will draw the nations to Him. Moved by desire they will climb Mt. Zion. There is a banquet table on top of this outstanding mountain. This is where the blessings and bounty of the Lord are waiting for His people:

> *"On this mountain the LORD Almighty will prepare a feast of rich food for all peoples, a banquet of aged wine — the best of meats and the finest of wines. On this mountain he will destroy the shroud [death] that enfolds all peoples, the sheet that covers all nations; He will swallow up death forever. The Sovereign LORD will wipe away the tears from all faces; He will remove the disgrace of his people from all the earth. The LORD has spoken."* — Isaiah 25:6–8

THE JUDGE OF THE NATIONS — 2:6–8

"He will judge between the nations and will settle disputes for many peoples. They will beat their swords into plowshares and their spears into pruning hooks. Nation will not take up sword against nation, nor will they train for war anymore. Come, O house of Jacob, let us walk in the light of the *LORD*."

The result of the great worldwide revival will be the justice of God coming to the nations. Divine wisdom will **"settle disputes for many peoples** (ethnic groups)." The Judge of the nations is coming in His church. When the Word of the Lord comes out of Zion the wisdom of he Lord will fill the nations and resolve ethnic conflicts, which divide and destroy. International disputes will be settled as the people stream to the mountain of the Lord's Temple.

Wisdom not warfare will come to the earth. The nations will learn wisdom from the lips of our Bridegroom-Judge. Converting weapons of war into instruments of harvest and fruitfulness, the nations will need no military training. There is a day coming when the harvest of the nations will supersede the wars and conflicts between people groups. The attention of the world will turn to the Great Arbitrator, Jesus Christ, the wisdom of God. It will be the time of walking "in the light of the Lord" as He dwells among His people.

"Plowshares" (ministries of harvest) will be utilized instead of strife and division. **"Pruning hooks"** (prophetic and apostolic ministries) will be functioning to set in place that which is lacking in the church. It will be a wonderful day when we lay aside our swords, which we have used against each other and take up the word and ministry of reconciliation (II Cor.5:17–21, James 3:16–17). The ministries of evangelism will bring rejoicing on this Mountain as the people of God learn wisdom and righteousness.

"Come, O House of Jacob, let us walk in the light of the LORD!" The Jacob life in us must submit to the light of the Lord. Our flesh life needs His Light to convert and transform us. His Light enables us to walk pleasing to God and prepares us for further revelation. Thankful for the morning light, He will bring us further into the noontime brightness. Faithful in little, He will entrust us with more. To him who has, more will be given. Come, all who are not yet perfect and struggle in the way … let us walk in the light of the Lord (Eph.5:8)!

MAN WILL BE BROUGHT LOW — 2:6–8

What happens if we refuse to come up the mountain of the Lord and learn His ways? What if the pride of man drowns out the voice of the Lord calling all men to repent and seek Him? What will take place? Will God overlook the rebellion of man? What follows is the mountain of men's pride in contrast to the Mountain of the Lord's Temple and how God will render judgment against every other mountain.

"You have abandoned your people, the house of Jacob. They are full of superstitions from the East; they practice divination like the Philistines and clasp hands with pagans. Their land is full of silver and gold; there is no end to their treasures. Their land is full of horses; there is no end to their chariots. Their land is full of idols; they bow down to the work of their hands, to what their fingers have made."

The Lord will abandon a people who persist in wickedness after repeated warnings (Prov.1:20–33, II Pet.3:8–11). Even though He may abandon a people, He will not abandon His *mercy* to those who love Him (Psalm 91). But if we refuse to hear Him who speaks from heaven and have a continual resistance to doing what is right, He will turn His back on them.

The nations of the earth are under the threat of God's judgment. Nations align themselves against God and against His righteousness. Every nation on earth is faced with the fact that God has and God will abandon a people who have turned their backs on holiness. What would cause God to abandon a people in judgment?

1. **The influence of false religions — "superstitions from the East."** This could describe our day with terms such as, New Age philosophies, practicing sorcery, divination, casting spells, witchcraft, relying on the control spirit operating through fear and manipulation, deifying man, and a broad minded tolerance that allows for every demonic influence. When we have a wall

up for God's ways and our walls down for all of these dark ways, we are tempting God to turn away from us. To mix the worship of the true God with superstitions and teachings from false religions will result in God abandoning us (Deut.18:9–11).

2. **Affluence without worship of the True God — "their land is full of silver and gold."** This is the lust of things, materialism, mammon worship, addicted to the stock market rather than prayer, greed, money-mad, lovers of things and pleasures more than lovers of God, luxurious living that produces a forgetfulness of God and eternity to come. **"There is no end to their treasures."** This is a description of blatant materialism that all for the comforts of the flesh. In this nation of treasures beyond counting, we should always remember that all good things come down from above. All our prosperity is so that the church may take the gospel to the nations of the earth, not to hoard for us! The Bible does not condemn wealth — God is concerned with how it is acquired, how it is used, and if it replaces Him as our security (1 Tim.6:6–10).

3. **Confidence in military might rather than God — "there is no end to their** (war) **chariots."** This involves the stockpiling of nuclear and conventional weaponry, etc. So much of the wealth of our nation is spent on military hardware and development of new weapons technology. Yet, in the time of battle ahead for America, only God can spare us. The time is now to turn to God and cry out for Him **Not** to turn against us and abandon us. All our weapons cannot defend us from the judgment of God.

4. **Idolatry, the worship of things made by men — "they bow down to the work of their hands."** Idolatry in America includes the love of human wisdom, our clever ideas and creations from man, the exaltation of man and what he makes (produces). The Hebrew word for **Idol** has as its basic meaning, 'worthless' or 'nothing.' The Hebrew word is *'elilim'* and the word used here

for God is *'Elohim'* — an obvious play on words. Our society is one of the most idolatrous ever. We make computers, cars, people, ideas, opinions, television, entertainment, and turn them all into little gods that we serve. How can what we make with our fingers be called divine? How absurd! What will all our **Things** do to save us in the coming Day of Judgment (Isa.10:3)? The worship of idols will culminate in the last days with the worship of the Beast, the Man of Sin.

As we race toward judgment, we can expect these 4 areas to increase and intensify. There are demonic forces energizing each of these 4 categories. Our battle is against those forces, *"the spirit of this world,"* not against other humans (flesh & blood). It is time to come out from all these things and be separated unto the Lord. There is a day when mercy steps aside and divine judgment is loosed on the earth. May the Lord stir us to seek Him while He may be found.

---

[20] The word "stream" means, 'to sparkle, to be cheerful.' In Isaiah 60:5 it is translated, 'radiant.' A cheerful stream of people will come into divine radiance as they come up the mountain of the Lord. This speaks of the supernatural uphill flow of the river of God bringing the nations into the Kingdom of Christ. This is the reversal of the dispersion of the people at Babel (Gen.11). Even Acts 2 is a preview of the nations coming together to Zion.

4

The Lord Alone Exalted

"The Lord alone will be exalted in that day...."

God will be exalted over everything He has made. Mankind will soon bow before Him, not their idols! America will be humbled, so she will seek God. The church will be humbled, so we will seek God. **You** will be humbled by the coming events, so **You** will seek God!

"So man (Heb. 'common man') **will be brought low and mankind** (Heb. 'men of importance,' i.e. leaders) **humbled — do not forgive them** (or, 'do not raise them up again')."

Shame, degradation and humiliation await those who forsake the ways of God. When human beings depart from the Lord they lose their dignity, their true humanity as those made in His image. **All** will be brought low (note the two Hebrew words for man in 2:9). **All** will be humbled before the presence of the Triune God. Those who bowed down to idols will now bow down to the Sovereign King and Judge of all the earth. This is not a bowing down of adoration, but of compulsion. Now there is mercy to bow in adoration, before the time of repentance is past....

The people who have lived in contempt of the glory of the Transcendent God will one day feel the weight of His punishment — they will bow down under it forever! His terrible judgments are coming! There is much we must learn about God's ways. As we go up to the Mountain of the Lord, He will teach us more of the Royal Ways of the King. As Judge of the Nations, He will by no means clear the guilty (Ex. 34:7). His judgments will be swift and sure. As the thunders of His judgments are heard in the nations, it will strike dread in the hearts of the lost.

THE TERROR OF JAH — 2:10–11

"Go into the rocks, hide in the ground from dread of the *LORD* and the splendor of his majesty![21] The eyes of the arrogant man will be humbled and the pride of men brought low; the *LORD* alone will be exalted in that day."

It will be too late for forgiveness. There will be no escape as the wicked face the dread of God head on. The Day of His wrath will one day come with no place to hide. Even the rocks and caves of the earth will not cover us from His gaze. Calvin, the theologian said, "This coming judgment is more to be dreaded than a thousand deaths." The awesome **Dread** of the Lord will fall as the **Splendor** of His **Majesty** begins to fill the earth. A new sense of holiness will fill the atmosphere of earth as His coming nears. All the Lord has to do to humble us, is show us the splendor of His glory.

Everyone on earth will seek to hide in a rock. Those who love the Lord will find shelter in the **Rock** of salvation. Those who deny the Lord will make the rocks and caves their hiding places from the face of God (Lit. 'hide in the dust from the face of the terror of the Lord'). People will long to seek refuge from the fierceness of His eyes, the fire of His gaze, the Sword in His Hands. What a fearful appearance of Yahweh! This **Majesty** will be the Majesty of God in judgment. As He is exalted over man in righteous judgment, the **Splendor of His Majesty** will be made known.

We have known His majesty revealed in grace, but have we seen His majesty revealed in judgment? What will He look like wearing the Robes of the Judge? Oh, the terrible reality of facing God in your sins! The only way to run from God is to run to **Him**. Mercy will cover you, but you better run to the Mercy Seat while you have time.

> Isaiah prophesies with the same intensity and in the tradition of Amos: *"Woe to you who long for the day of the LORD! Why do you long for the day of the LORD? That day will be as though a man fled from a lion only to meet a bear, as though he entered his house and rested his hand on the wall only to have a snake bite him. Will not the day of the LORD be darkness, not light, pitch-dark, without a ray of brightness?"*
> — Amos 5:18–20

"The eyes of the arrogant man will be humbled." The lofty, haughty, proud looks of mankind will be brought low (Prov. 6:16–19, 21:4). "The Lord alone will be exalted in that Day" Who would be able to stand in that day? Who would be worthy of receiving honor and glory from men? Who would be capable of declaring truth and righteousness that cannot be contested? The Lord **Alone**.

A DAY IN STORE — 1:12–18

"The *LORD* Almighty has a day in store for all the proud and lofty, for all that is exalted (and they will be humbled), for all the cedars

of Lebanon, tall and lofty, and all the oaks of Bashan, for all the towering mountains and all the high hills, for every lofty tower and every fortified wall, for every trading ship and every stately vessel. The arrogance of man will be brought low and the pride of men humbled; the *LORD* alone will be exalted in that day, and the idols will totally disappear."

In God's mind, days do not simply come around ... rather, each day is a distinct act of covenant-keeping (Gen.8:22, Ps.74:16). Every day is divinely planned and given forth to man. This is the day the Lord has made, each day. Within these sent days, there is a day in store, in reserve, that is especially the Lord's. It will be inserted at the point He alone has determined. On that day, all the **Pride** of man and **Arrogance** of human beings will be crushed. On that day, man's day will be over and the Lord Almighty alone will be exalted. He will be seen as **Jehovah Sabaoth**, the Lord of Hosts, the Lord of armies, the Lord Almighty!

The following terms are symbols of spiritual realities. It is a parable to describe strongholds within us that must be dealt with. It is a half-figurative, half-literal description of what will be brought down on that day Yahweh has in store for all the proud of heart....

"All the cedars of Lebanon, tall and lofty" — These cedars were particularly admired in those days as the noblest of trees. Solomon used them in building the Temple in Jerusalem (I Kings 5:6). Lebanon was seen as a symbol of beauty in the Scriptures. These tall and lofty cedars are a picture of men of high standing in society. Men are like trees that stand tall and upright, only to be cut down in death. Jesus stands as the fairest of all the trees, like an apple tree in the forest of humanity (Song of Songs 2:3). His incorruptible humanity is like the wood that was used in the forming of the Tabernacle and the Ark of Covenant, overlaid with gold. The tall and lofty cedars are the princes of the people who seem important on earth — they will all be brought low!

"All the oaks of Bashan" — These oaks were known for making oars (Ezek.27:6). They speak of military captains and soldiers that were like the savage bulls of Bashan surrounding Jesus on the cross (Ps.22:12). The brutal man will not stand before **Him**.

"All the towering mountains and all the high hills"—Governments and kingdoms of this earth are like hills and mountains. Even the highest of men's governmental authorities will bow to the One called the Lord Almighty!

"Every lofty tower and fortified wall"— This could refer to the strongholds in the mind of man, *"high thoughts that exalt themselves against the knowledge of God (II Cor.10:3–6)."* It speaks of military power and might (Isa.30:25). Towers and walls served as a refuge during an attack. Those who rebelled against God built a tower in Babylon (Gen.11:1–9, II Cor.10:3–6) seeking to be independent of God as their security. But there will be no defense from the wrath of the Lamb. There is no military might that will resist Him and His coming!

"Every trading ship and every stately vessel *(ships of pleasure)"* These are the largest of ships, able to take the longest voyages and the greatest cargoes. It speaks of the great commercial empires built by man (Ezek.28:2–5). We have mistakenly taken pride in our economic security and have exalted ourselves. The economic system, the commerce of earth will be brought down to the feet of Jesus as He establishes an eternal kingdom where righteousness and justice prevails. (The Hebrew for "Every trading ship" is literally — 'Every ship of Tarshish.' Jonah went on a ship to Tarshish to flee from the Lord — yet he was brought low to the belly of a fish! Saul of Tarshish was brought low to the dust when he met the Lord!)

All of the present order will be overthrown. Economic, military, governmental, personal. It will all come down like a tottering wall on the Day of the Lord! Like a whirlwind of wrath, the Lord's coming will be preceded by this terrible, fierce storm upon the lofty and proud of the earth. What words of terror for the unrepentant wicked!

What is our way of escape as believers in Jesus Christ? It is the way of the cross. The way of humility and lowliness before our Sovereign Lord and King (Rom.12:3, Eph.4:2). The Lover of your Soul is a Mighty King who holds a rod of iron in His hands.

"And the idols will totally disappear."[22] Who would cling to an idol when Jehovah comes in fury to overthrow the nations? Isaiah 17:7–8 states, *"In that day men will look to their Maker and turn their eyes to the Holy One of Israel. They will not look to the altars, the work of their hands, and they will have no regard for the Asherah poles and the incense altars their fingers have made."* It will be the end of man's day, and worship of what he has made.

THE COMING DREAD OF GOD — 2:19–22

The Lord is about to set Himself to action — rising up to shake the earth. Heb.12:25–29, *"See to it that you do not refuse Him who speaks. If they did not escape when they refused Him who warned them on earth, how much less will we, if we turn away from Him who warns us from heaven? At that time His voice shook the earth, but now He has promised, 'Once more I will shake not only the earth but also the heavens.' The words 'Once more' indicate the removing of what can be shaken — that is, created things — so that what cannot be shaken may remain. Therefore, since we are receiving a kingdom that cannot be shaken, let us be thankful, and so worship God acceptably with reverence and awe, for our God is a consuming fire!"* There will be no escape for the ungodly!

This is not just prophecy, it is history. God has judged the earth and the nations that turn away from Him. We have the account of the worldwide flood as a testimony of God's righteous judgments. Many will say, 'God would never do that.' But He has already and He will again.

"Men will flee to caves in the rocks and to holes in the ground from dread of the *LORD* and the splendor of his majesty, when he rises to shake the earth. In that day men will throw away to the rodents and bats their idols of silver and idols of gold, which they made to worship. They will flee to caverns in the rocks and to the overhanging crags from dread of the *LORD* and the splendor of his majesty, when he rises to shake the earth."

As our God rises to shake the earth, multitudes will throw away their idols of silver and gold as they seek natural and man-made shelters. Like Adam, man will run from the presence of the Lord. All that once was worshipped will be garbage to them. Rodents and bats will be surrounded with the golden treasures once esteemed by man. Thrown away in haste, mankind will have a reversal of values — suddenly faith in Jesus will be the only true escape and the things of earth will be discarded as meaningless! When the Lord rises to judge, men will creep into their earth-cellars....

Revelation 6:15–17 states, *"Then the kings of the earth, the princes, the generals, the rich, the mighty, and every slave and every free man hid in caves and among the rocks of the mountains. They called to the mountains and the rocks, 'Fall on us and hide us from the face of Him who sits on the throne and from the wrath of the Lamb! For the great day of their wrath has come, and who can stand?"*

"When He rises to shake the earth." There is a day in store when the Lord will rise to shake the earth. We have prayed for years for Him to arise ... and He will. But not the way we assumed. When He rises to shake the earth (and hearts of dust) there will be an abandonment of all that is of man. Everything that can be shaken will be shaken. So that what cannot be shaken will remain for ever (Heb.12:25–29).

"Stop trusting in man, who has but a breath in his nostrils. Of what account is he?" Our entire confidence must be in the uncreated **God** who made all things. Man's life is fragile and temporary. His breath is in his nostrils, ready to stop at any moment. With all our boastings and with all our ingenuity and marvelous inventions, man is but a poor, vain creature. In all our littleness and helplessness we must turn away from the answers of men and ask for the breath of God.

God had to breathe into man that breath of life — we do not exist by our own strength or in our own strength. Just as it was given, it can be taken away. Even the "little gods" that man pretends to be will be found trembling on that day. Man is nothing next to **God**! We have the Name of the **Lord** to trust in. As a loving Father we may come to Him and be saved from wrath. He is what we need and **He** is the One we should trust in.

[21] Lit. 'the terror of Jah, His Majesty's splendor'
[22] This verse has only three words in the Hebrew — 'nothings to nothingness.'

5

He Rises to Judge

"They have brought disaster upon themselves."

God's prophet continues to warn God's people of judgment to come. The prophetic task is to awaken the nations to the word of God. Jeremiah, Ezekiel, Noah, and Jonah were all prophets of God sent to warn and stir a nation. To remove the ministry of a watchman is a serious evil. It silences the trumpet that gives the certain sound of what God is about to do. Ezekiel was told to warn the people or he would be guilty of their blood on his hands (Ezek. 3). In these last days the prophetic warnings of God will be heard again in America.

God is about to systematically topple the nations of the earth and establish His eternal kingdom. God's government through the scepter of His Son will be established on earth just like it is in heaven. Everything that gets in the way of this Throne set on wheels of fire (Dan.7:9–10) will be consumed in His flames. The King is coming and He is a Judge who sees everything with eyes of holiness.

It is important for the church in America to hear the words of *"nevertheless, I have this against you (Rev.2:2–4, 13–14, 19–20)."* We must hear what the Lord has against us, not merely what He likes about us. True friendship is the grace to share with your friend what is wrong. As friends of God, the church must hear what the Lord may have against us.

Isaiah declares in Chapter three that the Lord's judgment will proceed against the rulers, the government of the nation. Chaos will be the resulting effect of the Lord's hand against them. Incompetent leaders will arise. Food and water will be taken from them; the morality of men and women will sink in the depths of degradation. Isaiah 3–4 gives us a picture of both judgment and glory being poured out at the same time. As the darkness intensifies upon the earth the light of Christ in His church will shine ever brighter....

We must not only understand God's principles of prosperity but also His principles of judgment. God's judgments restore His greatness in the eyes of mankind. When we exalt man, his accomplishments, the works of his hands, his government and wisdom, **God** is seen as insignificant. When we are big in our own eyes, God is small. *To exalt God is to humble man!* It is the prophet's job to exalt God. **Big God, Puny Man!** Judgment puts man back into his place (John 12:31–32). Judgment takes us to a place we don't want to go, but where His purposes are restored.

When God comes in judgment, wearing the robes of a **King** and **Judge** — man is insignificant, small and weak, mortal, stubborn, insubordinate, rebellious, proud and haughty, filled with arrogance and vanity. As God pours out the foreordained bowls of judgment on nations, the **Sovereignty Of God** is restored in the eyes of His people. The rebellious will curse God for being just, the righteous will magnify Him, even in judgment.... The day will come when the church will welcome the judgments of God and pull them to the earth with their prayers of declaration. God wants the church to participate with Him in ruling and reigning — and that includes judgment.

The nations of the earth are on a slippery slope, inviting the judgments of God. The only hope for the earth is a repentance that is sincere, resulting in a change of heart and a change of course.... If America does not repent, the same scenario that happened in Judah, will happen in the USA! Our hope is in the One who will hear our cry of repentance and spare us, if we turn to Him!

What does it look like when the Lord rises to shake the earth? We can see it in history with the Babylonian invasion of Israel and we can see it in front of our eyes today: The Sovereign God will take away every thing that makes one feel safe and secure.

WHEN A NATION BREAKS DOWN — 3:1–7

As the Lord rises to judge the nations He forewarns before He comes. He tells us ahead of time what His judgments will look like. As moral chaos and social anarchy come to a people, they must understand that it is not their political leaders that hold the answer, but the One who rises to judge! Here is what judgment looks like when it comes:

"See now, the LORD, the *LORD* Almighty, is about to take from Jerusalem and Judah both supply and support:[23] all supplies of food and all supplies of water."

"Supply" — The Lord will take away our false confidences in economic stability. Shortages of all kinds, but especially of food and water. They become scarce and precious. Famine is soon to come.

(Food and water also speak of fresh words from God & measures of His Spirit). The pillars of a nation are its "supply and support." The Lord Almighty is about to take from the nations that reject His Word, "all supplies of food and all supplies of water." Perhaps we can learn from even our present day that God will do this, and He will do it in America if we do not repent.

"Support" — God's judgment will take the form of removing from a nation their noble men, heroes, warriors, judges, prophets, counselors, elders, captains, etc. Military, civic, and religious leaders will be removed as a nation copes with who will govern. Creature comforts and creature confidences will be taken away by God. With every prop removed, the nation will have nothing to lean on anymore. The nation that turns from God will face this judgment. Men and women of noble heart who are the standard of righteousness for a nation, even they will be removed. When the breakdown of a nation comes they will be taken away as a judgment from God.

"The hero **('mighty man')** and warrior **('generals')**, the judge and prophet, the soothsayer **('the prudent')** and elder **('the wise')**, the captain of fifty **(officers)** and man of rank **(leader)**, the counselor **('wise statesman')**, skilled craftsman and clever enchanter **(eloquent orator)**." **These are the military, civic, and religious leaders who will prove to be inadequate when the Lord rises to judge the earth.**

"I will make boys their officials; mere children will govern them." — Incompetent administrators will arise to take their place. The ruling elite will be merely youths who have no remedy or solution. It is a blessing to a nation when the elders rule the land.

"People will oppress each other — man against man, neighbor against neighbor. The young will rise up against the old, the base against the honorable." **The oppression of civil government will intensify; 'big brother' will take the place of common compassion.**

Civility is removed and social chaos takes over. Even the wise and honorable are set aside, replaced by the wicked and selfish. Oppressive laws take the place of mercy and justice.

"A man will seize one of his brothers at his father's home (ancestral aristocracy), **and say, "You have a cloak** (a fine garment that is a sign of wealth and influence), **you be our leader; take charge of this heap of ruins** (fallen buildings)!" **But in that day he will cry out, "I have no remedy. I have no food or clothing in my house; do not make me the leader of the people."** The people will look everywhere for something or someone they can trust in, but no one can be relied on. Government crumbles so a corrupt and chaotic government is established, with the inexperienced and unstable.

This is the definition of anarchy. As they ignore the **One** who is the **True** leader they are left with those who have no remedy. There is a Righteous King who has a cloak of righteousness to give them if they would be turn to Him! Society and human government will be called "this heap of ruins" as total devastation of society results.

One of the most important things for our times is to hear the Word of the Lord through His prophets in the Scriptures. The principles of impending judgment are clear, waiting for us to seek them out. Listen to Ezekiel's description:

> *"When terror comes, they will seek peace, but there will be none. Calamity upon calamity will come, and rumor upon rumor. They will try to get a vision from the prophet; the teaching of the law by the priest will be lost, as will the counsel of the elders. The king will mourn, the prince will be clothed with despair, and the hands of the people of the land will tremble. I will deal with them according to their conduct, and by their own standards I will judge them. Then they will know that I am the* **Lord**." — Ezekiel 7:25–27

EVIL WILL ABOUND — 3:8–12

"Jerusalem staggers, Judah is falling." Jerusalem and Judah represent the people of God. The word "staggers" is the literal word, 'overthrown,' — a city overthrown. The word for "falling" is 'ruined.' Even the righteous will be shaken when the Kingdom of God overtakes the earth. The message of Isaiah is this: **It Can** happen here! Do not think you will escape because you live among a people who once knew the Lord. To turn your back on God is to invite His judgments.

"Their words and deeds are against the *LORD,* defying his glorious presence." Their words and deeds against the Lord stood as a testimony against them. Their lives were "defying ('provoking') the glorious presence[24] of the Lord." By their sins the holiness of God was provoked. God sees crime, divorce, abortion and the evil of humanity as a violation of His holiness — it is against the Lord. Do you think the Righteous King will not judge the sins that defy His glorious presence? Is He blind? Will He not judge unrighteousness? Where is the fear of God? Will we really get away with our sin?

"The look on their faces testifies against them." With impudence written all over their faces God could see what they were doing in the shadows. The brazen-faced-culture of ours makes a disgrace of what is right and parades in public what is evil. **"They parade their sin** [gay parades?] **like Sodom; they do not hide it. Woe to them! They have brought disaster upon themselves."** Unashamed they paraded their homosexuality, refusing to even blush with shame (Jer.3:3). Their openness becomes their boast; refusing even to cover up their sin it is flaunted publicly. This blatant exposing of wickedness brings disaster upon themselves (diseases, judgments, etc.)

> *"Your wickedness will punish you; your backsliding will rebuke you. Consider then and realize how evil and bitter it is for you when you forsake the* **LORD** *your God and have no awe of Me, declares the* LORD, *the* **LORD** *Almighty."* — Jer. 2:19

Our own wickedness will punish us. We don't need the devil to do it. Our own backsliding will rebuke us. We don't need a preacher to do it for us. The sting and pain of our own sin is the punishment we face when we forsake God and have no awe (fear) of Him.

"Tell the righteous it will be well with them, for they will enjoy the fruit of their deeds." They will enjoy the sweet fruits of seeking God and serving His kingdom. They will reap the good seeds they planted, for seeds turn into fruit. The fruit of their deeds is the holy confidence that God is with them, even in a season of judgment. We can know it will go well with us, even when destruction is poured out on the nations. The message of hope is this: "Tell the righteous it will be well with them." Judgment is coming, persecution is coming, but for those who hope in the Lord, it will be well.[25] Even if we face the valley of the shadow of death, we know that He is with us and will bring comfort and peace to our soul.

"Woe to the wicked! Disaster is upon them! They will be paid back for what their hands have done." Woe to the wicked! Isaiah uses this phrase 22 times (one time he used it about himself!) The fruit of their deeds will be disaster, and it will overtake them! All the darkness of human imagination is nothing compared to the dread and destruction that will come upon the wicked. For they have been planting seeds over years that will one day be reaped. Bad seeds will bring forth bad fruit (Gal.6:7–8).

Judgment is payback time. What you have planted, what you have invested, will be given back. The Lord comes with His reward with Him. If you have planted good seeds and good deeds, you will be rewarded with blessing, honor, and glory. You will eat the fruit of the seeds you have planted years ago. However, if you have planted wickedness and sowed the seeds of dark ways and compromise, when the Lord comes, He will bring you the reward of your deeds — disaster and destruction!

"Youths oppress my people, women rule over them (a reference to queen-mother or ladies of the harem). **O my people, your guides lead you astray; they turn you from the path."** Even the children ('little ones') will be evil and oppressive; perpetrating unspeakable works of darkness. Generational curses will come back to haunt society. Juvenile delinquency will take on new levels of wickedness. Men will abdicate leadership roles to women and the leaders will lead the people into greater darkness (*lit* 'leaders have swallowed up the way'). The leaders keep others from knowing and following the good ways of God.

HE ENTERS INTO JUDGMENT — 3:13–15

"The *LORD* takes his place in court; He rises to judge the people. The *LORD* enters into judgment against the elders and leaders of his people." The Lord arises in judgment — He 'stands up to judge' the leaders and the people. We have prayed for God to arise and He will. He will arise in judgment.

> *"Rise up, O God, judge the earth, for all the nations are your inheritance."* — Psalm 82:8

It is wrong to assume that when God arises in judgment it will not affect the church, the godly on the earth. When judgments fall, there will be the righteous who will be swept away with the wicked. When the Titanic sank, there were believers in Christ who perished. When earthquakes and famines come, there are true believers who will perish. Judgment affects us all and we must prepare our hearts not to be offended with the ways of God. Yet even in a time of judgment we are to tell the righteous, "it will be well with them." We must tell the brothers and sisters not to give up or lose hope. Our prayers will be heard and judgment can be averted.

To the corrupt leaders and to the people who follow them the Lord speaks: **"It is you who have ruined my vineyard** (persecuting the church, the source of joy/ wine for the earth); **the plunder from the poor is in your houses** (making themselves rich by oppressing the poor). **What do you mean by crushing my people and grinding the faces of the poor? Declares the** **Lord, the** ***Lord*** **Almighty."**

> *"Do not exploit the poor because they are poor and do not crush the needy in court, for the* Lord *will take up their case and will plunder those who plunder them!"* — Proverbs 22:22–23

The Haughty Women of Zion — 3:16–26

"The ***Lord*** **says, "The women of Zion are haughty, walking along with outstretched necks** (proud will), **flirting with their eyes** (vision, understanding), **tripping along with mincing steps** (dancing with the world), **with ornaments jingling on their ankles** (to attract other lovers). **Therefore the Lord will bring sores** (making them unclean and unable to come before God as priests — Lev.13:2–6) **on the heads of the women of Zion; the** ***Lord*** **will make their scalps bald." In that day the Lord will snatch away their finery: the bangles and headbands and crescent necklaces, the earrings and bracelets and veils, the headdresses and ankle chains and sashes, the perfume bottles** ('houses of the soul,' or lust) **and charms** (superstitious amulets), **the signet rings** (emblem of authority) **and nose rings, the fine robes** ('festival garments,' formals and tuxedos) **and the capes and cloaks, the purses and mirrors, and the linen garments and tiaras and shawls."**

Moral disintegration results from the judgments of God and invites the judgments of God. This passage describes the vanity of a nation being removed ... and the vanity of the church! It is the sins of the church that will invite judgment on a nation. The "women of Zion" are a picture of the church, the bride of Christ. It is an indictment against the haughty churches that exalt themselves in the Day of the Lord. Instead of humility, purity, single-mindedness, the churches of Zion are described as "haughty," flirtatious with the world, enjoying the things of the world but not the things of God We are to become a Bride adorned with the jewels of beauty and holiness for our Husband, Christ Jesus (Isa. 61:10, Rev.21:2) and not an erring bride that flirts with other lovers and seeks to win the world with charm and vanity.

When God judges a nation for the vanity and pride of the church, we will no longer care about how we look to others. Twenty-one items of jewelry and adornment are mentioned, but they will all be removed and stripped away. When bombs drop and judgment falls we will not be going to shopping malls to buy fine clothes, sniffing the fragrances and passing by the jewelry counters — nor will we seek to impress the Babylon system of this world. **"Instead of fragrance there will be a stench** ('rottenness')**; instead of a sash, a rope; instead of well-dressed hair, baldness; instead of fine clothing, sackcloth; instead of beauty, branding** ('blisters')**."**

Judgment will snap us out of our infatuation with the world and take us where we have been unwilling to go ... the place of humility! Instead of fine fragrances the land will have "a stench" (decaying bodies?) Instead of beautiful sashes and adornments, "a rope." No more beauty shops, only "baldness" (nuclear fallout?) Instead of fine wardrobes, only "sackcloth." The boast of beauty will be replaced with "branding" (skin diseases or radioactive burns?) God is about to strip the vain thinking from our nation and reverse our value systems. What we have sought for will be stripped away. Self-confidence will be replaced with humiliation and bereavement.

Even our military might cannot save us when God rises to judge the earth. "Your men will fall by the sword, your warriors in battle." We cannot expect God to defend a disobedient and rebellious people. Never has there been a nation more ripe for judgment than America. It can happen here. Sadly, the church of today walks about with pride and an outstretched neck, prancing forward with the theology that we are too good and too important for God to judge....

"The gates of Zion will lament and mourn; destitute, she will sit on the ground." This is what will happen when the young men of a nation are destroyed in judgment. The gates of Zion, the very foundations of the church will lament and mourn. We will begin to see that it is the pride of a nation and the pride of the church that has invited judgment, bringing death to our **"warriors in battle."**

Spiritual protection over a nation and over a church is lifted by impurity and sin. The Lord has the remedy for this, for He will remove the guilt of the women of Zion. It will take the Spirit of judgment and the Spirit of burning to do this, but the Faithful God will accomplish His work.... In Isaiah 49 we see the restoration of the daughters of Zion as her sons return to her (49:14-26). True spirituality and authentic humility will soon be the most sought after virtue on the earth. When the church walks in these virtues we have light to offer to the nations.

---

[23] This is a play on words similar to, 'bag and baggage' or 'house and home.'
[24] Lit. 'the glance of His glorious eyes' (See Habakkuk 1:13). Sin provokes the glorious eyes of God. This is the opposite of finding favor in His eyes.
[25] This is not a guarantee that the righteous will not perish in the wars, famines, earthquakes and plagues, which are coming. But it is a promise that God will be good, kind, faithful, and loving no matter what comes!

6

The Branch of the Lord

"Over all the glory will be a canopy."

With vast and grand themes Isaiah is unrivaled in all of Scripture as a description of cataclysmic judgments, the survival of a holy remnant and the canopy of glory that is coming to earth. There will emerge a cleansed, holy people in Zion. The Lord Himself who becomes one with His people. They will be the outgrowth of the One called the Branch — they will posses His glory and His beauty.

This chapter reads like a 'Table of Contents' that previews what is discussed throughout the remaining chapters. All the themes of Isaiah are found in seed form in this passage. Lest we begin to believe that Isaiah is negative or simply a thundering voice of judgment, notice the positive and glorious themes he presents here in Chapter 4:

Revival of the church	**v.1**
Removal of disgrace	**v.1**
The Branch of the Lord	**v.2**
The Beauty and Glory of Christ	**v.2**
The Fruit of the Land	**v.2**
The Boast of the Survivors	**v.2**
New levels of holiness	**v.3**
Removal of filth from the church	**v.4**
Cleansing of bloodstains	**v.4**
The Spirit of burning desire	**v.4**
The Cloud of Holy Smoke	**v.5**
The Glow of Flaming Fire	**v.5**
A Canopy of Glory	**v.5**
A Shelter or Tabernacle	**v.6**
A Supernatural Hiding Place	**v.6**

How surprising and shocking will be the saving word of God in the last days. When all the nations are in despair and the shaking of everything on earth intensifies, the **Work** of God will take place as He brings glory to His Bride. What looks like *judgment* to the wicked will look like *glory* to the redeemed. To the evil doers on earth He will appear as the Terrifying Judge, but to His Bride He will be seen as the Glad Bridegroom coming for His wedding day!

"In that day seven women will take hold of one man and say, "We will eat our own food and provide our own clothes; only let us be called by your name. Take away our disgrace!"

This is a continuation of Chapter Three regarding the women of Zion. There is coming a day when the church will become so destitute of answers and agendas that she will turn to one Man, the Lord Jesus and take hold of Him. We have taken hold of the world and we have taken hold of clever ideas, but the seven women (seven churches — see Revelation 2 and 3) are about to lay hold of their Beloved. The longing of the church will be for Him. We will want to be called by His great Name. The shadow of His beauty will remove our disgrace and make us a worthy partner to labor with Him.

THE BEAUTIFUL BRANCH — 4:2

"In that day the Branch of the *LORD* will be beautiful and glorious." The Branch of the Lord is understood by nearly every serious Bible student as a term for the Messiah, the Lord Jesus Christ. He is the Righteous Branch that springs forth with an ever-increasing life.

In the Hebrew language the word for "Branch" is a nominalized verb (a verb that is changed to a noun, i.e. the 'rising' of the sun) and could be translated ... the **'Sprouting'** of the Lord, or the **Branching Forth** of the Lord. Like a sunrise that increases and intensifies, like a sprout that begins small and grows and grows to full stature ... these thoughts are all included and wrapped into the Hebrew word for the **Branch Of The Lord**.

> *"The days are coming, declares the* **LORD**, *when I will raise up to David a righteous Branch, a King who will reign wisely and do what is just and right in the land."* — Jeremiah 23:5

This is the Immanuel character of Christ that increases and grows like a branch carrying His life (Isa.9:6–7). Jesus is the Fruit Bearing Branch from the stump of Jesse (Isaiah 11). His branching forth with fruit and power speaks of the restoration of the Davidic kingdom. Our Family Tree is the Branch of the Lord in His beauty. As He increases in His church the fruit bearing Christ, will sprout forth with a power and a glory that will eventually cover the earth.

The actual Hebrew word for the Branch is 'Nazer,' which is the root word for Nazarene, Nazareth, or Nazarite (See Matt.2:19–23). The Heavenly Branch Man, Jesus, the Nazarene, has now come to branch over our sin and the self-life to become our true source of power. He will continue to branch out in you until the Adam nature is overcome!

We see this **Branch** theme through the Scriptures as the Shepherd's Rod, the King's Scepter, the Rod of Moses, the Rod of Aaron that budded in a picture of resurrection life — and in the **Lampstand**. The Lamp stand in the Holy Place was a burning bush of gold with 7 branches giving light and revelation to the priests.

The seven branches were made from one piece of gold. So the church today is formed from One Branch, the Golden One, Jesus Christ. The ornaments on each branch were crafted from three stages of fruit bearing … buds, blossoms, and almond fruit. The three branches on each side (total of 6) each had three representations of each of the three stages of fruit. The central shaft (Jesus is the Center or the Vine) had 4 each and the other 6 branches had 3 each of the different stages of fruitfulness.

Here is the equation:

- 3 stages of fruit X 3 = 9
- (9 Fruit of the Spirit — Gal.5:22)
- 9 fruit per branch X 6 branches = 54 fruit
- Fruit of the central shaft = 12

54 + 12 = 66 Books of the Bible. His Word is a Lampstand unto our feet and a Light to our path! The Fruit of the Lampstand is the Revelation of the Word of God.

The church is the **Branch Man**, a many-membered representation of Jesus Christ on the earth. He that overcomes is the **Branch Man**, the One Body, the One New Man, the church. As He sprouts forth in us, the kingdom of God will increase until the nations of the earth and the kingdoms of man **All** become the kingdom of our Lord Jesus!

"Listen, O high priest Joshua and your associates seated before you, who are men symbolic of things to come: I am going to bring my servant, the Branch." — Zechariah 3:8

"The Branch of the LORD will be beautiful!" The very life of Christ coming forth in His people will be seen as beautiful and glorious! How beautiful is Jesus? How radiant does He appear to the angels and to the worshippers around His throne? This Beautiful Branch will spring forth, bringing glory to His people. Those who once had a frenzied pursuit of beauty in chapter 3:16–18 will touch the true beauty of the Branch Life of Jesus Christ.

THE FRUIT OF THE LAND — 4:2–3

"And the fruit of the land will be the pride and glory of the survivors in Israel." Jesus is not only the **Branch** of the Lord, He is the **Fruit** of the earth. Jesus had two natures, one **Divine** and one **Human**. He is Yahweh's Branch and David's Branch. As the Branch of the Lord He is the Holy and Divine Son of God sprouting forth from heaven, as the Fruit of the earth He is the Son of Man with an earthly, human body made from the same dust as ours. **Jesus** is the fruit of the earth, the fruit of the womb of Mary, the Fruit on the Tree of Life, the Fruit of the Spirit in a body, the **Fruit** of God's life in full expression. He is both **Branch** and **Fruit**.

The prophet Isaiah saw a day in which the Branch of the Lord with excellence and splendor will branch out from His place (the church) and bring forth the fruit of restoration and purity. Christ in His Deity, in His Holy Beauty will be the boast of an end time people.

Jesus is going to Branch out from His throne into the lives of a people who have honored and magnified His Name. The Son of God is going to be multiplied and reproduced in His people. As a **Man** with the Divine Life, He is a **Seed**, a grain of wheat to produce many grains through His death and resurrection (Isa.53:2, John 12:24). As His life comes forth in the church, the **Fruit** of the earth will be seen in you and I (Isa.27:6)! All of this will be ushered in by God's judgment of the earth! The issues of judgment are what will bring forth the sprouting of the Lord in His people!

All that Jesus is, He is for His people. He is beautiful and glorious **For You**. He is in you to sprout forth, to bring forth the fruit of His life ... until He becomes your glory and dignity and splendor and beauty.

Jesus makes human life attractive and honorable. Come forth in me, Lord Jesus. Let my heart be a womb that gives birth to a new expression of your Fruit on the earth! This is the revelation of the New Testament — God's life inside bearing fruit outwardly in our humanity.

For too long, *we* have tried to be the pride and glory of the earth. Our human lives, our plans, our church programs, our exaltation of man has sought to be the pride and glory ... but the day is coming when the Branch Man, the Fruit of the Earth will become the pride and the glory. All our boast and confidence and glory will be found in Him. The Divine Glory is about to dwell with us!

The word **"survivors"** can also be translated 'escapees,' 'remnant,' or 'refugees.' The devastation of coming judgment will not annihilate God's people; it will release the life of the Branch and the Fruit of the earth into His church. War and judgment will grow the church into the image of Christ. Tribulation works for us, in bringing forth mature sons and daughters. For the survivors, their glory will be in **Him**. The Word of God prophesies there will be a time when the remnant of the land will be beautiful in the Lord, adorned with His excellence and strength. Jesus will be their admiration — to those who believe He is precious (I Pet.2:7) and the fairest of 10,000 (Song of Songs 5:10).

> *"Once more a remnant of the house of Judah will take root below and bear fruit above. For out of Jerusalem will come a remnant, and out of Mount Zion a band of survivors. The zeal of the* LORD *Almighty will accomplish this."* — Isaiah 37:31–32

"Those who are left in Zion, who remain in Jerusalem, will be called holy." Paul takes this terminology and applies it to the last days when the church is *"caught up"* to be with the Lord (I Thess. 4:17). A **Holy Remnant** will remain — they will have been spiritually changed and become a Holy expression of the Lord. In a way yet to be explained, they will be carrying the glory and holiness of the Lord.

God always leaves a nucleus of heaven on earth, even in judgment. We assume nothing will be left, but God brings His purpose forth out of a remnant of survivors. How many times a move of the Spirit begins but falters, yet out of the holy remnant, God begins again. He may drown the world, but He will leave a seed to build an altar.

What about **"all who are recorded among the living in Jerusalem"** — who are they? There are many "books" mentioned in Scripture — here is a Book of Destiny that contains the names of those survivors who become holy to the Lord. Perhaps this is the same book Daniel wrote about in Daniel 12:1. Or it could be the book David mentioned — *"All the days ordained for me were written in your book before one of them came to be"* (Ps.139:16). Moses spoke to the Lord about His *"book"* (Ex.32:32). We read also of the *"Book of Life"* (Ps.69:28, Phil.4:3, Rev.20:12) which belongs to the Lamb (Rev.13:8). For those who fear the Lord, there is kept a *"scroll of remembrance"* with their names written within (Mal.3:16). Jesus reminded His disciples that their true source of joy was not that they could cast out demons, but that their names were written in heaven (Luke 10:20).

THE SPIRIT OF JUDGMENT —THE SPIRIT OF FIRE 4:4

"The Lord will wash away the filth of the women of Zion; He will cleanse the bloodstains from Jerusalem by a spirit of judgment and a spirit of fire."

What will make this remnant holy? What will purify those who are left? It will require a purging from the Lord to "wash away the filth of the women of Zion." The Hebrew word for filth is also translated in the Old Testament as a drunkard's vomit (Isa.28:8) and human excrement (Isa.36:12). What a picture! The women of Zion (local churches) are filthy and needing to be washed by God. Our blasphemies and uncleanness must be purged. We must not be those *"who are pure in their own eyes and yet are not cleansed of their filth (Prov.30:12)."*

Remember these truths about Zion:

1. **Zion is a term for God's people** *(Isaiah 51:16)*
2. **God's people dwell in Zion** *(Isaiah 10:24)*
3. **The Lord has chosen Zion** *(Psalm 132:13)*
4. **Zion is a term for the heavenly Jerusalem** *(Heb.12:22)*
5. **God dwells in Zion** *(Psalm 9:11)*
6. **Jesus, the King of kings, sits on the holy hill of Zion** *(Psalm 2:6, Zechariah 14:9)*
7. **Zion is the city of the Great King** *(Psalm 48:2)*

The women of Zion were haughty in Chapter 3, adorned with their expensive jewelry — now they are humbled and repentant, needing the cleansing of the Lord. But the gracious promise from God is found in Zechariah 13:1 — *"On that day a fountain will be opened to the house of David and the inhabitants of Jerusalem, to cleanse them from sin and impurity."*

This wonderful fountain filled with blood was opened up on Calvary's hill, releasing the power to cleanse from guilt and sin. How thankful we are! The blood of Christ has sterilized our hearts!

By the Judging Spirit and by the Burning Spirit, the filth of the churches of Christ will be washed away — even bloodstains! The Spirit[27] will come first to judge, then to burn. The Holy Spirit brings judgment to His church by giving us the discernment to know what is pure and what is vile.

This **"Spirit[28] of judgment"** releases holy vision to see things as God sees them. Decisions will be made by the justice of God, not the prejudices of men. It is not that He merely executes judgment, but that He gives **Discernment** to see what is holy and what is not. It is a Spirit of **Conviction** that will bring the church to **Justice** and purity. We will be convicted by the Spirit of God (Spirit of Judgment) when we err from God's ways.

The **"Spirit of *Fire*"** ('burning') will thoroughly cleanse God's remnant and make them holy by refining fire (Mal.3:2–4). It is a fire of passionate love for Jesus Christ that will cleanse the church. The Holy Spirit is invigorating our hearts to seek out intimacy with God and become best friends with Jesus. A flaming zeal will accomplish this. The fire of love as a seal over our heart will keep us pure from temptation and end time distractions. The burning heart for Jesus will burn out the filth of a worldly spirit.

A CLOUD AND A GLOW — 4:5–6

"Then the *LORD* will create over all of Mount Zion and over those who assemble there a cloud of smoke by day and a glow of flaming fire by night; over all the glory will be a canopy. It will be a shelter and shade from the heat of the day, and a refuge and hiding place from the storm and rain."

In the midst of this testing time of tribulation the promise of God remains — He will be our Guard and our Guide! "Tell the righteous, it will be well with them" (Isa.3:10). The Lord will be our defense in a time of trouble. After He has cleansed us with justice and fire, He will "create over all of Mount Zion and over those who assemble there (or, 'its assemblies) a cloud of smoke by day and a glow of flaming fire by night."

All the congregations of believers (even two or three gathered in His Name) shall be taken under the special protection and care of heaven. They will no longer be scattered or disturbed — they will be under the same glory cloud that led Israel through her wilderness. A cloud of smoke by day will screen them from the scorching heat and the glowing of flaming fire will keep them warm and enlightened through the night (Ex.12:21, Neh.9:19). Great is our God![29]

God will dwell among us! This is what the cloud of smoke and glowing fire is all about — the presence of the Lord. These are the sights you see in the Throne Room — smoke and fire! Abraham went into a trance and saw the Lord pass between the cut halves of the sacrifice as a smoking pot and a flaming torch (Gen.15:17). In the days of Moses, the Lord camped among them but was inaccessible to the people, His glory was too overwhelming — but now in the fullness of His glory, there is open access to His shelter, His tabernacle.

"Over all the glory will be a canopy. It will be a shelter and shade ... a refuge and hiding place from the storm and rain." Jesus is both the Canopy and the Tabernacle. He is a Canopy to cover the people of God and He is a Tabernacle to provide refuge for God's people. This canopy is the 'huppa,' the Hebrew marriage canopy. It always denotes the marriage chamber. God and man are going to be joined in a great wedding, the marriage of the Lamb! **Revival** is going to break out at this time! The Heavenly Bridegroom is going to come to dwell with His eternal Bride, the Church.

Over all the glory of that day will be stretched out a tent or canopy. This marriage chamber will provide peace, rest, and security for the Bride. The Stronger Man has come to the earth to be with His Beloved. In a time of stormy rain, there is a Shelter, a Refuge, a Hiding Place to run into.

Isaiah the prophet tells us that in the last days a canopy of glory will cover regions of the earth like a 'tabernacle' or shelter from the judgments that will come. The word for **"shelter"** is the very word used for David's Tabernacle (Amos 9:11). This is a prophecy of an emerging refuge on earth, 24-hour a day Houses of Prayer with continual worship and intercession forming 'glory-tabernacles' over regions and cities.

In the New Testament Church of today, we are not looking for a literal re-building of a tent or tabernacle, or even the rebuilding of the Temple, but the spiritual fulfillment of Davidic worship released in the Body of Christ through the anointing of the Holy Spirit. It is Christ in His church singing and praying and dancing, as the Root of David.... These prayer furnaces will release into the atmosphere the very cloud of glory that led Israel through her time of testing and trial in the wilderness. The symbols of the book of Exodus will be reappear in the last days!

Listen to how the Moffat Translation renders this:

'Then, shading all Mount Zion, the Eternal Himself will form a cloud during the day time, and spread over all the gatherings there a canopy of brilliant light, a fire within the night, to shade them from the scorching heat, and safely shelter them form storm and sleet.'

Truly, the best days for the Bride of Christ are yet to come!

---

[26] See Zechariah 6:9–13 — This **Branch Man** will be clothed in majesty and will sit and rule on a throne as a priest, A **King-Priest**. In Rev.1:5–6 & 5:9–10 believers are clearly described as kings and priests.

[27] The Hebrew word for Spirit can also be translated 'breath' or 'blast.' The blast of judgment and the blast of fire!

[28] Or, "by the *breath of judgment*."

[29] In the last days there will be a return of the working of creative miracles seen in the book of Exodus!

7

The Singing Prophet

"I will sing for the One I love!"

Isaiah is a singing prophet, most prophets are. Music and the Spirit of Prophecy go together like Light and the Word. This chapter contains three prophetic songs: The Song of the Vineyard, the Song of Woes, and the Song of Judgment. What a variety of methods God will use to awaken His people, and bring sinners to repentance!

For some it will be the sweet songs of love (Song of Songs), for some it may be like the prophetic song of Moses found in Deuteronomy 32, for others still, it will be a sorrowful lament. John the Baptist came and played the funeral dirge but the people would not mourn. Jesus came and played the flute of rejoicing, but

Deuteronomy 32, for others still, it will be a sorrowful lament. John the Baptist came and played the funeral dirge but the people would not mourn. Jesus came and played the flute of rejoicing, but the people would not dance (Matt.11:16–19).

Sometimes God will speak plainly and 'get in our face.' Other times He will speak in parables or pictures, prose and in verse. In Chapter 1 the Lord has tried to reason with us. He wants us to listen to Divine logic. But here, He states His case in a poem, a song.

The prophet sings this song to the glory of His Beloved. Maybe it was sung by Isaiah at the Feast of Tabernacles as the grape harvest was brought in. Or perhaps Isaiah walked through the streets of Jerusalem or the hillsides of Israel singing to God's people a prophetic message. Or perhaps the Lord Jesus sang this over Jerusalem as He stood on the hillside overlooking the city, weeping (Luke 19:41).

THE ONE I LOVE — 5:1–7

"I will sing for the One[30] I love!" The prophet is determined to sing this song. It is the Holy Spirit singing through him of the One loved by both the Father and the Spirit. The words "I will" are the language of emphatic determination in the Hebrew ('I will sing indeed!') Hebrew scholars are convinced that this is one of the most rich and eloquent poetic masterpieces in the entire Bible. It is a Divine song of the "One I love." The prophet's Friend is Jesus Christ. The prophet's heart comes forth as he chants his melody to the King and His vineyard.

The chief characteristic of this song is lament. Because the vineyard disappointed the Lord, the song disappoints us. It is not entertainment and would likely never be popular to hear it sung. It is teaching a word that brings the Lord's heart to us. Do we really only want to hear what is popular and pleasing to our flesh, or do we want to hear God speak, even if His words are meant to adjust us?

Isaiah's song is the parable of Jehovah's vineyard on a fruitful

Jesus our Lord planted this vineyard.[32] **"My Loved One had a vineyard on a fertile hillside."** The hill is very fruitful, receiving the rays of the sun and the rains from heaven. The Hebrew is literally, "My Loved One had a vineyard on *the horn of the son of oil* (or 'fatness'). An anointed hill is the vineyard of the Lord! It is a strong way of saying God's people are anointed and called His Sons of oil. The Holy Spirit has made us fertile and rich in God. We are all 'sons of oil' with the life of Christ within us.

The location of this vineyard was all that one could desire for a vineyard. So is our position in Christ, we are His sons and daughters of oil, located on the high and heavenly places of God's Spirit. The Owner who planted this vineyard could expect from the vines planted on this hillside of oil, to produce only the finest of grapes.

> *[What about America? What more could God do for our nation that what He has already done. He has blessed the vision of our founding fathers, He has poured out His rich treasures upon us until we have become the envy of the world. We have a financial prosperity that is staggering when compared to the poor of this world. We have freedom, we have favor from God. He has stood with us in times of war and times of difficulty — God has blessed this nation. But what fruit is being produced from this fertile hillside?]*

"He dug it up and cleared it of stones and planted it with the choicest vines." Digging around this vineyard to build a stone fence of protection, the Lord has cared for His people, His vineyard. He has cleared it of stones, removing all that would make His people stumble (Isa.62:10). For the Church, He has removed our stony heart and given us a heart of flesh to respond to His voice. For Israel, these stones would represent the Canaanites, those inhabitants of the land that made them stumble. Then He planted and established His people, calling them the choicest ("noblest") of vines — with everything they needed to grow and be fruitful.

the land that made them stumble. Then He planted and established His people, calling them the choicest ("noblest") of vines — with everything they needed to grow and be fruitful.

Jeremiah 2:21 echoes this thought, *"I had planted you like a choice vine of sound and reliable stock. How then did you turn against Me into a corrupt, wild vine?"*

"He built a watchtower in it and cut out a winepress (wine vat) **as well."** For Israel, this watchtower would be Jerusalem. The place where the Owner of the Vineyard dwelt and cared for His vineyard. For the church, the watchtower is Zion, the place of His presence.[33] He not only planted us as His vineyard, He dwells among us (II Cor.6:16). The winepress or wine vat is the sacrificial system that God gave to His people to provide them with access to God. For you and I, the wine vat is the privileges of open access that the Holy Spirit (our wine!) is to us as we gather together....

All of these privileges, but still, **"only bad fruit"** or literally, 'stink-fruit' was found. This is the fruit of our corrupt nature. How the Lord wants to make us into **His** image, bearing His fruit! Look again at all this Vine Keeper has done for His vineyard:

- **The location was excellent**
- **The soil was fertile.**
- **The vines were the best.**
- **A fence of protection was laid around it.**
- **All the stones were cleared away.**
- **A watchtower was erected.**
- **A wine vat was built.**

"What more could have been done for my vineyard than I have done for it?" God is seeking to show that He is doing the **Right Thing** when He sends judgment. He is speaking to our conscience. He compels His people to agree with His standards, His wisdom, and

"Judge between me and my vineyard." The prophet Nathan brought a parable to David, Isaiah brings this parable to us! You decide for yourself.... Is God right to withhold His blessing from such a vineyard?

The local church is a vineyard that is meant to produce wine and release the life and joy of the Holy Spirit — this is the kingdom of God. The local church is also compared to a wineskin that is to contain a constant flow of new wine and dispense the life of the New Covenant to the people of God....

- ➢ The Vine & Branches is Christ & His Body.
- ➢ The Fence/ Wall is God's presence built by praise.
- ➢ The Tower is the 5-fold ministries of Eph.4:11.
- ➢ The Winepress is the ministry of the Holy Spirit

"I will take away its hedge, and it will be destroyed; I will break down its wall and it will be trampled. I will make it a wasteland.... I will command the clouds not to rain." Witness the determination of God.... **"I Will"** is used five times in these three verses!

"The wall" — **Intercessory Prayer**.

"A wasteland" — **What We Become** when God lifts His blessings from us.

"The clouds no longer give rain" — the **Ministry Gifts** will no longer pump us up.

"Briers and thorns" — part of the curse of our fallen flesh.

Where God once pruned and cultivated and cared for His vineyard, He now will neglect them just as they had neglected Him. The very blessings and gifts they enjoyed would now be removed in judgment. The obedient are preserved, the wayward will be destroyed. This parable is a message we must give heed to and take warning. The

God who has blessed our nation and kept us, will turn from us in judgment if we do not repent.[34]

> *"Therefore, I have begun to destroy you, to ruin you because of your sins. You will eat but not be satisfied; your stomach will still be empty. You will store up but save nothing, because what you save I will give to the sword. You will plant but not harvest; you will press olives but not use the oil on yourselves, you will crush grapes, but not drink the wine.... Therefore I will give you over to ruin and your people to derision; you will bear the scorn of the nations."* — Micah 6:13–16

Yet in the midst of all this, the love of God for His people resounds as He defines them as **"the garden of His delight"** or 'the plant of His pleasantness!' With mercy He speaks, even when He judges! He will come looking for justice and righteousness, for love believes the best (I Cor.13:7). With expectation He waits in hope that a people which had received blessings beyond number would bring forth righteousness and justice.

"He looked for justice, but saw bloodshed; for righteousness, but heard cries of distress." The prophet uses another play on words: Instead of **"justice"** ('mishpat'), they brought forth **"bloodshed"** ('mishpak'—violence). Instead of finding **"righteousness"** ('tsedaka') He heard the groaning of **"distress"** ('tseaka'). It gives Him no delight to find bloodshed among us as He hears our cries of distress (those wrongly oppressed). But not even these cries will cause Him to turn away His hand of judgment (Prov.1:24-33).

> *"But the LORD Almighty will be exalted by his justice, and the holy God will show himself holy by his righteousness."* — Isaiah 5:16

[30] This is the name David, or Beloved. Jesus Christ is the heavenly David, beloved by all who know **Him**.

[31] Compare Jesus' parable of the vineyard in Matt.21:33–45 and the psalmist's allegory in Psalm 80:7–19.

[32] This applies to both Israel and the church. Obviously, Israel is the vineyard of the Lord. But in John 15, the Vine and His Vineyard are applied to the Lord Jesus Christ and His redeemed people, the Church. Throughout the gospels we see the people of the Lord compared to a vineyard (Matt.20:1, 21:28–41, Mark 12:1, Luke 13:6, 20:9–16, John 15:1).

[33] For the intercessor, there is a watchtower within you! God has placed the grace upon you to see, hear, and pray in the will of God.

[34] See II Chron. 36:14–21; Ps.89:40–41, Isa.7:23–25, Ezek.15:6–8.

8

The Song of Woes

"THE HOLY GOD WILL SHOW HIMSELF HOLY."

God desires to pluck out of our hearts the accusation that God is cruel when judgment strikes. We cannot understand why God would strike the earth with His wrath and destroy the peoples. Yet, it is only mercy that has allowed us to live on His earth in our sin and wickedness. So what follows is the logic of God as He seeks to help us process Divine judgment.

Isaiah speaks 6 'woes' upon the people who have forsaken a life of righteousness. What follows is a description of the wild grapes God's vineyard had produced. These are dangers to avoid for the Lord's people ... for they will bring 'woe' into our lives:

GRASPING MATERIALISM — 5:8–10

"Woe to you who add house to house and join field to field till no space is left and you live alone in the land."

Because the heart of man is not content with what we have, we grasp for more. This covetousness can result in ignoring the cause of Christ and forgetting justice for the oppressed. The implication is these properties were taken unjustly from the poor, encroaching on the rights of their neighbors and taking their land (Micah 2:1–2).[35] A monopolizing of possessions for our greed is sin. We are a people who don't know when we've had enough! The more we have, the more we want to have!

"The LORD Almighty has declared in my hearing...." The prophet heard the clear voice of the Lord as He uttered these words. Isaiah overhears the councils of judgment.... **"Surely, the great houses will become desolate...."** No matter how great or protected we may seem, when God rises to shake the earth, even the **"great houses"** of man will become desolate!

It is the prophet's solemn duty to speak the Word of the Lord as He gives it. There is no mention of how the people responded to these 'woes' but we can imagine it was not too favorable. The Spirit of God can give His servants boldness to confront and point out the sins of God's people. This is the valid exercise of the anointing of the prophet (Isa.58:1).

"A ten acre vineyard" is literally, 'a ten-yoke vineyard' (what could be cultivated by 10 yoke of oxen — possibly more than 10 acres). A substantial piece of land would only produce about six – eight gallons of wine from its grapes. Six bushels of seed would produce less than a half a bushel of seed crop. Their greed may move them to take the land of others, but it will not give them fruit or satisfaction. This would be the judgment of God released through this **"woe."** The land-hungry would end up being hungry, in spite of their land.

DRUNKEN PLEASURE SEEKING — 5:11-17

"Woe to those who rise early in the morning to run after their drinks, who stay up late at night till they are inflamed with wine."

This is a woe spoken over those in pursuit of intoxication — sensual indulgence over spiritual intimacy with God. Drinking is their life![36] They make drinking their business. Its what gets them out of bed in the morning and keeps them up all night long. The true intoxication of the human spirit is found in total abandonment to the Holy Spirit! Strong drink will blind the heart from heavenly pursuits and deceive the hearts of men. For the people of this world, 'Life is a party!' Many are those who feel 'Since the Titanic is sinking; we'll just live it up until we die.' This is all part of a Babylonish system that is destined for destruction (Rev.18:22).

Their 'raves' are great with hot music and dancing.... **"But they have no regard for the deeds of the Lord, no respect for the work of His hands." No Regards** means they saw some of what God was doing, but did not value it! **No Respect** means they did not grasp the significance and importance of God's works. Many are those who do not esteem the power, wisdom, grace and compassion of our God. He is only seen as an angry Father. The lie of the serpent has lodged in the human spirit, corrupting every thought about the God of heaven. All the time we abuse His goodness, we ignore His miracle power, we take for granted His mercy. We take the good things He gives us and make them fuel for our fires of lust and greed.

No regard, no respect.... His hand is lifted up in judgment but they will not see it! They will not disturb themselves in their pleasures. They cannot believe God has a controversy with them. Bartender, another drink!

But strong drink leaves mankind without spiritual perception. Blind to the realities of life, the drunkard plunges headlong into destruction. Judgment, death, eternity in hell, facing a Holy God in your sins … none of these things matter if only there is enough booze to go around!

"Therefore my people will go into exile for lack of understanding." God will judge **His** people and send them into exile for not perceiving His holy ways and the coming Day of Judgment! The understanding we lack is the understanding that God is Judge and He will not acquit the guilty. He is about to wear the Judges Robe and visit the earth to execute justice.[37]

"Men of rank" is literally 'men of glory.' Since thirst for strong drink was their downfall, they will thirst in exile. The land will spew out the drunkards, they will all be taken into captivity; hunger and thirst will be their portion.

"Therefore the grave (Sheol) **enlarges its appetite and opens its mouth without limit."** Because of the sinfulness of earth, the grave grows hungry — stretching wide its mouth to receive all of the slain of the earth. A great monster with wide-open jaws — this is the picture that Bible paints of the grave. The Hebrew word is 'Sheol' or the underworld. The grave has an appetite that is grows in a time of judgment (Prov.30:15–16, Hab.2:5). It is a monster we have summoned up by our sins. The multiplied wickedness of the earth causes the underworld to accommodate those who will make it their home. Yet, Paul wrote of a day when death is swallowed up in victory at the appearing of Jesus to the earth (I Cor.15:54).

The destiny of man is to be brought low, not made like gods. All of mankind will be humbled by the display of judgment to come. Even the most arrogant of men will be made low. Our vain accomplishments will crumble someday. All of this is so that the **"LORD Almighty will be exalted by His justice, and the holy God will show Himself holy by His righteousness."**

Justice exalts God. Injustice is a reproach and a dishonor to our Creator-King. When we truly long to see God exalted, we will long for justice on the earth. The judgment that brings man low will lift

God high. Do you want God to be exalted in the earth? Do you want the peoples of the earth to learn the righteous ways of the Lord? Do you really love the beauty and holiness of the Lord? Be prepared beloved to see the hand of the Lord lifted in judgment. The Omnipotent One who controls nations, the Lord of Hosts **Will** manifest Himself as glorious, as holy, as true in all His judgments. He is a God of irresistible power — none can stand in His way when He arises to shake the earth!

> *"When your judgments come upon the earth, the people of the world learn righteousness."* — Isa.26:9

When you see His judgments fall, He is showing Himself **Holy**, not just mad. When the Lord punishes sin, He is seen as holy. When Ananias and Saphira fell over dead for lying to Peter, God showed Himself holy among them!! Judgment is a display of His righteousness, not just His wrath. The Hebrew word for Holy means separated. God is separated from all others by the greatness of His holiness. He is a God of unspotted purity. Righteousness is His holiness expressed.... Holiness in action for all to see.

What was once a vineyard has now become a grazing place for lambs. The desolation has been complete. The party's over! Now the meek ones (lambs) will inherit the earth.

DEFIANT SINFULNESS — 5:18–19

"Woe to those who draw sin along with cords of deceit, and wickedness as with cart ropes."

The third 'woe' is spoken over those who drag their sins along with them like a beast harnessed to a cart, dragging it by the ropes of deceit (falsehood). By holding on to what is false they bind themselves to their own bondages. **"Cords"** turn into **"cart ropes."** Can you see the inhabitants of the earth from God's viewpoint? Dragging along our sins like the heaviest of burdens ... straining and tugging our way through life. *"The evil deeds of a wicked man ensnare him; the cords of his sin hold him fast.... But the LORD ... has cut me free from the cords of the wicked."*[38] Only God can break these chains!

By their habits, they are hardened in their sins and cannot be free from them. Slaves to sin (Rom.6:16) they are unaware that what they are dragging along with them will one day consume them and drag them into hell. This bondage leads to arrogance, demanding that God prove Himself, doubting that God is at work, they are blind to seeing the works of God all around them. It is deceit and falsehood that keeps the world trapped, loving darkness rather than light (John 3:19).

"Let God hurry, let Him hasten His work (the timing for judgment) **so we may see it. Let it approach, let the plan of the Holy One of Israel come, so we may know it."** Some are so defiant they taunt God with cries to 'Bring it on! We can take your fury! This is the same language of the last days mockers that Peter prophesied would come:

> *"You must understand that in the last days scoffers will come, scoffing and following their own evil desires. They will say, 'Where is this coming he promised? Ever since our fathers died, everything goes on as it has since the beginning of creation. But they deliberately forget that long ago by God's word the heavens existed and the earth was formed out of water and by water. By these waters also the world of that time was deluged and destroyed. By the same word the present heavens and earth are reserved for fire, being kept for the Day of Judgment and destruction of ungodly men."* — II Peter.2:3–7

Listen to Jeremiah's commentary —

> *"They keep saying to me, 'Where is the word of the LORD? Let it now be fulfilled!"* — Jer. 17:15

> And Ezekiel's proverb — *"Son of man, what is this proverb you have in the land of Israel: 'The days go by and every vision comes to nothing'? Say to them, 'This is what the Sovereign* LORD *says: I am going to put an end to this proverb, and they will no longer quote it in Israel.' Say to them, 'The days are near when every vision will be fulfilled. For there will be no more false visions or flattering divinations among the people of Israel. But I the* LORD *will speak what* **I Will**, *and it shall be fulfilled without delay. For in your days, you rebellious house, I will fulfill whatever I say, declares the Sovereign* LORD." — Ezekiel 12:22–25

Fallen man does not want to believe the truth of coming judgment. Our hearts resist the holy and sovereign ways of God that bring man low and raises up the Son of God. They are challenging God to appear in judgment! Woe to those who mock the Holy One of Israel.

IMMORAL PERVERSION — 5:20

"Woe to those who call evil good and good evil, who put darkness for light and light for darkness, who put bitter for sweet and sweet for bitter."

Irreverence and great wickedness are close partners. All moral distinctions are blurred when our hearts are hardened to God. We can even become those who **"call evil good and good evil."** Convinced that darkness is light and light is darkness, they plunge further into moral chaos. Refusing the value system of heaven, they embrace the value system of hell. Sin becomes an accepted way of life!

Not content to abandon what is good, they must label it as evil. When you abandon the absolute standards of God's law, you will find a reversal of every true virtue. Good is mocked and evil is embraced. Light is ridiculed and darkness is worn like a cloak. The sweetness of God is called bitter — the bitterness of sin is called sweet.[39] Evil is justified, even applauded. The heart of man is prejudiced against what is pure.

There is a **Vast** difference between good and evil, between light and darkness. God has separated them and defined them in Genesis 1. **Perversion** is the very essence of sin. We twist truth to fit our immoral definitions. We begin to define good and evil by our actions, not by God's Holy Word. Choosing darkness, choosing evil — the heart of man is filled with darkness.

ARROGANT CONCEIT — 5:21

"Woe to those who are wise in their own eyes and clever in their own sight."

Pride is at the root of all sin. The fifth woe of the prophet is uttered against the vanity of man who presumes they are **"wise in their own eyes."** True wisdom is found in God. Those who say they are wise but leave out the fear of God, are foolish and arrogant. To neglect the true source of wisdom leaves open only one other source — the wisdom from the darkened should of man.

> *"Do not be wise in your own eyes; fear the LORD and shun evil. This will bring health to your body and nourishment to your bones."* — Proverbs 3:7

The Lord would remind us: *"The wisdom of the wise will perish, the intelligence of the intelligent will vanish"* (Isa.29:14). We all want to live without having to seek the Lord for wisdom. We want autonomy from God. We substitute our cleverness for crying to Him, and our intelligence for true Spirit-given discernment. We consider ourselves able to get out of messes and disprove the wisdom of God. Who will outwit Eternal Wisdom? Who can outsmart Infinite Intelligence? God will resist the proud of heart. We must "come down" like Zaccheus from our tree of self-righteousness and meet Jesus on street level.

There is a wisdom that coming from above that is without pride. It flows into teachable, humble hearts and imparts heavenly insight (Jam.3:13–16, Prov.11:2). As God unveils His Son as the One in whom is hidden all wisdom and knowledge, the cleverness of the wise will be confounded.

CORRUPTION OF JUSTICE — 5:22–23

"Woe to those who are heroes at drinking wine and champions at mixing drinks, who acquit the guilty for a bribe, but deny justice to the innocent."

Notice the world's version of success! The heroes and champions of the ungodly are bartenders! Their boast is in their ability to mix drinks! Their drunkenness causes them to pervert justice for the poor. This denial of their rights leads to judgment from the God who sees. Drunken judges who boast in their pleasures and drunkenness. Taking bribes to pervert justice. Justifying the guilty and denying the rights of the innocent — these sins will provoke the fires of God's judgment to burn.

SONG OF JUDGMENT — 5:24–25

When God's judgment falls, sinners will not endure! With decaying roots and withering flowers they will be swept away. Just like dry grass falling helplessly into the fire they will be rejected by God. They have rejected the Law of the Lord Almighty and spurned the Word of the Holy One (Prov.13:13).

"The Lord's anger burns against His people." God's anger is a righteous anger. It is the necessary vindication of the honor of His holiness & authority! There is no reason for you to make an apology for God's anger. It is not a blemish on the Divine Character and it is not inconsistent with His mercy and grace. His anger is as pure and holy and good as His mercy or as His love. Everything about God is holy and perfect. (Deut.32:39–41, Ps.7:11–13).

There are as many references in the Bible to the anger, the wrath and judgment of God as there is to the love of God. Holiness requires a holy anger toward all that defiles and corrupts. The wrath of God is as much a perfection of His character as mercy, kindness and love.[40]

Divine anger is His holiness stirred up into activity against evil. Mankind will be made to feel the awesome Majesty of His holy anger. Not a malicious retaliation, but a vindication of His Word, His honor, and His authority. *"The wrath of God is being revealed from heaven against all the godlessness and wickedness of men who suppress the truth by their wickedness"* Romans 1:18.

Here are ways this righteousness is revealed:

- **The sentence of death passed upon all men.**
- **The banishment of Adam and Eve from Eden.**
- **The flood of Noah.**
- **The destruction of Sodom and Gomorrah.**
- **The wilderness wanderings of Israel.**
- **The destruction of nations in world history.**
- **The judgments of His people (Ananias — Acts 5).**
- **The reality of an eternal hell.**

When we truly understand the anger of God there will be changes in our hearts. We will no longer view sin lightly, gloss over it, or excuse it. The Holy Fear of God will be birthed within us. We will be quick to help others escape — "Flee from the wrath to come." It will make us appreciate and cherish even more the work of Jesus on the cross.

"His hand is raised and He strikes them down." That hand had been raised up many times to strike their enemies. Now it is stretched out against His own people. The Lord is slow to anger, but when it is kindled, there will be no escape. Who knows the power of His anger?

"The mountains shake, and the dead bodies are like refuse in the streets." The judgment is so severe that there is no one with strength to bury the dead. His wrath will one day shake all the mountains of the earth. "Yet for all this, his anger is not turned away, his hand is still upraised." God's fires of judgment will burn as long as there is chaff and sin to be fuel for it. Still His wrath is not exhausted. What will it be like on that judgment day when the Lord rises to shake the earth?[41]

HIS BANNER OF JUDGMENT — 5:26–30

"He lifts up a banner for the distant nations.... Here they come swiftly and speedily." With the power of heaven God will raise up a banner as a rallying point for the hostile nations. The summons of the Lord will go forth as He whistles for the nations to come and execute his judgments on His people. It is said that beekeepers can whistle and stir up a hive of bees to bring them back from the fields. So the Lord will whistle and call the nations to **Come**. God has two banners ... a banner of love over His Bride and a banner of judgment for a wayward people. Which banner would you want to live under?

The nations are God's servants. The course and destiny of nations is in God's hand! One is raised up to fulfill His purposes and others are raised up to execute His judgments, and fulfill His counsels. He will muster the armies of the earth to come against those who have resisted His will. Swiftly and speedily they will run to do the errands of holiness! How swift and speedily have we run to do the will of God?

There are times when God will anoint our enemies to be instruments of judgment against us. **"Not one of them grows tired or stumbles...."** Their progress is not impeded by natural failure.

Although coming along distance, they will not be a weary enemy! They are so eager for battle they do not even sleep! **"Their arrows are sharp, all their bows are strung...."** Their equipment is effective and sharp, at the ready, not subject to wear and tear, capable of great speed! They are ready to attack!

"They growl as they seize their prey and carry it off with no one to rescue." Like a roaring lion who carries off to safety its prey, on the prowl, ready to pounce with no one to deliver them. If God has turned away from a nation, who could stop the armies of judgment?

"Even the light will be darkened by the clouds." Unrelieved gloom falls upon the land. First like a lion, then like the sea — judgment sweeps over them leaving nothing but darkness and devastation. Judgment must finish its work!

Beloved, what you see in this passage is *what Jesus went through* for you and I. God will ultimately triumph in mercy — for all those who come to Jesus Christ!

---

[35] This would also be a violation of the principle of the Year of Jubilee, when debts were to be forgiven and land returned to its original owners.
36 Drunkenness will ruin a life. Prov.20:1,23:29–35, Job 21:12–18
[37] II Kings 24:14–16, Hosea 4:6–11, Amos 6:5–7.
[38] Prov.5:22 & Ps.129:4
[39] Bitter and sweet ... these are things usually left to private taste. But God has authority to speak to all matters of our life — even the things we view as private or discretionary.
[40] There is a time when our Friend will become our Foe if we reject His mercy. Isaiah 63:9–10
[41] See Isaiah 9:12, 18–19

9

The Throne Room

"High and exalted!"

This chapter is considered Isaiah's prophetic commissioning. But it holds more than just the way God calls a prophet, but how God brings hope to the world. For five chapters, Isaiah really didn't have much good stuff to say about Israel, the people of God, their destiny, etc. He had just prophesied six 'woes' upon the people he ministered to. It was at this point the Lord opened the heavens and showed Him the Throne Room.

Without a vision of the Throne Room all we have to say is what is wrong. We don't have true answers until we see the Lord high and lifted up … and our lips are cleansed! Isaiah had to learn that only a vision of the holiness of God could change the human condition.

This more than just the call and commissioning of the prophet. It brings us to the real solution of coming judgment and the devastation of the human heart. It is a **Holy** God revealed to our eyes, and the cleansing of our hearts and lips for ministry.

We must have the 'Isaiah 6 experience' take place with thousands of God's servants in coming days. If we see what Isaiah saw, we can speak what Isaiah spoke.... Pray for the revelation of the throne room if you dare!

"I Saw the Lord!"

This is a vision of **incredible grandeur**. Isaiah saw the very glory of God — the Lord seated on His throne, high and lifted up. He heard the solemn chanting of the seraphim. He felt the earthquake shaking the very foundations of the Temple. He witnessed the rainbow glory robe of Almighty God. He saw for himself the Holy Smoke of Glory in the Throne Chamber Room. There was an altar, fire, burning coals, flying seraphim and shaking thresholds.

This Vision of the Throne had a profound effect upon the prophet. He would never be the same again! His prophetic ministry from this day forward would be an overflow of that vision. He preached for years without a vision of the Throne — working hard for God but without a fresh vision. But from here on, he will speak of the hope of the world ... Immanuel!

After Isaiah saw the Lord, he pronounced his 7th Woe — upon himself!! The intense light of holiness began to pierce him through and through! The cry of holy echoed in his ears. He saw his life of uncleanness flash before him. How could see all of this and survive. How could He dwell with everlasting burnings!

"In the year that King Uzziah died." This vision came to Isaiah in the same year that King Uzziah died. Many scholars believe that Isaiah was the nephew of King Uzziah and had access to the royal palace. He knew the story of his uncle as well as anyone. What was so significant about Uncle Uzziah? His story is found in II Chronicles 26:1–21....

> *"All the people of Judah took Uzziah, who was sixteen years old, and made him king.... Uzziah was sixteen years old when he became king, and he reigned in Jerusalem fifty-two years.... He did what was right in the eyes of the* LORD*.... He sought God during the days of Zechariah, who instructed him in the fear of God. As long as he sought the* LORD*, God gave him success. He went to war against the Philistines and broke down the walls of Gath, Jabneh and Ashdod. He then rebuilt towns.... God helped him against the Philistines ... and his fame spread ... because he had become very powerful. Uzziah built towers in Jerusalem ... and he fortified them. He also built towers in the desert and dug many cisterns.... He had people working his fields.... Uzziah had a well-trained army.... The total number of family leaders over the fighting men was 2,600. Under their command was an army of 307,500 men trained for war, a powerful force to support the king against his enemies. Uzziah provided shields, spears, helmets, coats of armor, bows and slingstones for the entire army. In Jerusalem he made machines designed by skillful men ... to shoot arrows and hurl large stones. His fame spread far and wide, for he was greatly helped until he became powerful. But after Uzziah became powerful, his pride led to his downfall. He was unfaithful to the* LORD *his God, and entered the temple of the* LORD *to burn incense on the altar of incense. Azariah the priest with eighty other courageous priests of the* LORD *followed him in. They confronted him and said, "It is not right for you, Uzziah, to burn incense to the* LORD*. That is for the priests, the descendants of Aaron, who have been consecrated to burn incense. Leave the sanctuary, for you have been unfaithful; and you will not be honored by*

the **LORD** *God." Uzziah, who had a censer in his hand ready to burn incense, became angry. While he was raging at the priests in their presence before the incense altar in the* **LORD's** *temple, leprosy broke out on his forehead. When Azariah the chief priest and all the other priests looked at him, they saw that he had leprosy on his forehead, so they hurried him out. Indeed, he himself was eager to leave, because the* **LORD** *had afflicted him. King Uzziah had leprosy until the day he died. He lived in a separate house — leprous, and excluded from the temple of the* **LORD**."

Uzziah was a God-fearing king who prospered greatly as long as he sought the Lord. He started reigning at 16 and reigned for 52 years. He was a good king who built cities, developed agriculture and commerce, extended their national boundaries; he fortified Jerusalem and raised up a powerful military. God marvelously helped in all his enterprises until Uzziah became a strong and powerful king. His name means, 'Mighty is Jehovah! Power of Jah! Glory of Jah!'

Everything about Uzziah was to glorify Yahweh. But when he was strong and powerful, his heart was lifted with pride. He assumed a place before God that was not his. He offered incense as though he were a priest. *"But after Uzziah became powerful, his pride led to his downfall. He was unfaithful to the* LORD *his God, and entered the temple of the* LORD *to burn incense on the altar of incense."*

Only priests were allowed into the Holy of Holies to burn incense. The High Priest Azariah and 80 others tried to convince him it was wrong. As he stood there arguing with the priests, they saw a white patch of leprosy break out on his forehead. God had smitten him for his sin. Uzziah became the leprous king! He was secluded as a leper until the day he died.

"I saw the *LORD*!" It was in the year that Uzziah died, Isaiah saw the Lord. The prophet realized that God would judge even a king if he sinned. Isaiah saw the holiness of God in the judgment of the leprous king and knew that if good uncle Uzziah would be judged, then he would too. Isaiah was dealing with a holy God! We all want to see His face and spend time with heaven's King, but it is when we see the way He deals with sin that are eyes pop open and we really see the **Lord**.

Often, acts of judgment do bring a new revelation of God. In a crisis, we get a glimpse of the Lord of Glory that we did not have when living in ease and comfort. A spirit of repentance is released as God judges leaders over nations! The prophet could see himself in God's light as he saw the king being judged. When we see God's searchlight on others, it will cause us to judge ourselves also. **The Flesh Of Man Is The Corrupt, Leprous King That Must Be Judged!** The old order has ended; we must have a vision of our true King! *[If you can see the death of that 'proud king' who lives in you it will release a fresh vision of the Sovereign King.]*

"Seated on a throne, high and exalted"

What did Isaiah see? He was taken out of his body in his spirit to see the heavenly Temple of the Most High. "I saw the Lord seated on the Throne, high and exalted." Incredible! The Lord, high and lifted up, reigning as King on a throne! The heavens were opened as the prophet gazed on the glory of the King. Isaiah saw the Lord Jesus Christ! John 12:41 — *"Isaiah saw Jesus' glory and spoke about Him."* This was an appearance of Christ before His incarnation … the Eternal Word and Only Begotten Son!

- **A Throne of Glory**
- **A Throne of Government**
- **A Throne of Judgment**
- **A Throne of Grace!**

"The LORD is in his holy temple; the LORD is on his heavenly throne." — Psalm 11:4

This throne[42] was high and exalted over everything in heaven and earth. Conspicuous in power and authority, He is a sovereign King lifted up on this throne. No matter what is happening on earth, the Lord is at rest and in control! The Lord seems to be saying, 'Don't look down at the situation, or you will be disappointed and negative. Look up to Me. I am still here and still in charge. People are fallen, I am lifted up. Israel's king dies, but the God of Israel lives. An earthly throne might be vacant, but I, the Lord, still reign on high!'

"And the train of his robe filled the temple!"

The long, loose, flowing robes or skirts of His Robes filled the Temple with no room left for anyone to stand. "And the train of His robe filled the temple."[43] It is a scene of glorious majesty. Breathtaking! This royal robe is a picture of the splendor of his virtues. All of His virtues are bright and shining and pure. Joseph had a coat of many colors, but Jesus has a robe of every color and every dazzling virtue of God.[44]

In preparation for the work God had for His prophet, Isaiah must be overcome by this vision! Glory burning in awesome display, holy smoke filling the Temple with the threshold shaking and quivering at the display of the Splendor of Christ. **Isaiah Saw Jesus' Glory!**

THE BURNING ONES — 6:2–4

"Above Him were seraphs (seraphim)." Seraphim means 'the burning ones, fiery beings (taken from Hebrew word meaning 'set on fire' or 'to kindle.' Described nowhere else in Scripture, they are seen as guardians of the holiness of God — anointed, fiery custodians of the Throne Room. Winged creatures that swirl around the throne — ignited by the burning presence of Almighty God. These celestial beings had faces, feet, hands, they spoke in human language and they covered themselves with their six wings. These are the shining ones who burn with holiness. They fly close to the flame of Jah and are ignited in His presence! Burners! Holy Burners for Yahweh![45]

With three pairs of wings, they fly over the throne and echo the voice of the Lord. **"With two wings they covered their faces** (humility at the sight of God), **with two wings they covered their feet** (reverence), **and with two wings they were flying** (availability, service, ready obedience)." We are not told how many there were, or how huge they may have been, only that they used their wings to cover themselves in humility and reverence. Although they were beautiful, they were gazing on One of Infinite Beauty. Their supreme task was to hide themselves before the Face of the One on the Throne.[46]

With wings folded upward and wings folded downward, they would appear to Isaiah as huge flames of fire! If these exalted and glorious creatures, greater in power than anything Isaiah had ever seen, if they were unable to gaze upon God's Pure Holiness as they hid themselves **How Could God's People Seek To Display Themselves!** We want others to see if we are serving God, we want them to know that we have a gift. But Isaiah was coming under conviction as he saw the activity of the seraphim. He realized his ministry had been self-inspired, not ignited from this sacred flame of Jah! In covering their feet, they disavowed any intention to choose their own path. So must we let the Lord direct our steps as we humbly fly before Him!

Don't think this vision was only for the sake of Isaiah, *it is happening right now* in the throne room of heaven. The seraphim are still proclaiming the glory of God and are still hiding themselves from the face of Majestic Holiness. God wants us to see what Isaiah saw!

Moses' face shined with the glory of God as he dwelt forty days in the presence of the Consuming Fire. Stephen's face once glowed like an angel. God's messengers, His prophets, are meant to be like these burning ones. He makes His messengers flames of fire (Ps.104:4, Heb.1:7). Like the seraphim, they are to be God's attendants, those who fly near to the flame and have been kindled with the fire Jesus longs to send to the earth! Those who behold the Lord and have been ignited in His presence will be the world changers and history makers. **We Are To Burn In Holy Love!**

Filled with a zeal for His glory and His hatred of sin, God's 'burners' will ignite the world. They will become His living embers, and blazing coals. In humility, they will provide 'covering' for the Body....

"And they were calling[47] to one another." The Hebrew states, 'this one cried to this one'. Can you picture the seraphim on every side crying out in antiphonal song — responding to the revelation of Glory! Greater than the sound of any choir or symphony, the seraphim sang their continual song of holiness! Their one unbroken task is to praise and magnify the transcendence of God....

"Holy, Holy, Holy is the Lord Almighty." One Hebrew scholar states that the root word "holy" (kadosh) in Hebrew means both 'bright' and 'separated.' This is the very sense the apostle Paul taught by describing God as One who dwelt in *"unapproachable light."* I Tim.6:16

We have learned to live with unholiness so long, we have little idea of what holiness really is. We are undisturbed by the uncleanness of our lives and our lips. A new channel must be cut through the desert of our hearts to allow the sweet waters of holiness to flow, and heal our sin-sickness. Hear this truth: God is **Holy, Awful, Fearful, Majestic, Mighty, Transcendent**. Ex.15:11 says He is *"majestic in holiness, awesome in glory, working wonders."* The seraphim are crying out — **'Bright And Separated, Bright and**

Separated, Bright and Separated Is The Lord Almighty!' Holy sums up all His attributes.[48]

Power is God's arm, omniscience His eye, mercy His heart, wisdom His mind, eternity His age, but holiness is His beauty! God is Transcendent and Holy, separate from all His creation. He does not conform to a standard of holiness, **He Is** the standard of holiness. He is over and above all that He has made. He is free and completely independent from all that is evil. His eyes are so pure He cannot even look upon evil. There is nothing like Him and therefore cannot be compared adequately to anything! As Creator and King, He is separated from sin as far as brightness is separated from darkness. There are no degrees of holiness with God. No honest man could say, 'I am holy.' We must hide our 'unholiness' in the wounds of Christ.

The seraphim burst forth in song with the very essence of God's nature. His holiness is a combination of all of His virtues together in one glorious expression. Whenever the heavens are opened, you will hear this song of praise to the God Above All. We worship at His footstool, for the Lord is Holy! Why is the word **Holy** uttered three times? He is infinitely Holy, perfectly Holy, forever Holy! Our God is Father, Son, and Holy Spirit. God is the three-fold Holy One! The more they sing it, the more they see, which makes them sing more, which makes them, see more....

[42] Isaiah speaks of this throne 7 times — 6:1, 9:7, 14:13, 16:5, 22:23, 47:1, 66:1.
[43] Or, 'His trailing robes spread over the Temple floor' — Moffat translation.
[44] This very robe of glory has touched us in Christ When we "put on Christ" we are robed in His splendor before God and angels.
[45] Many believe these celestial seraphim are the "living creatures" mentioned in Ezekiel 1 and Revelation 4.
[46] Some see a parallel with the cherubim who cover the Mercy Seat with wings touching.
[47] The two seraphim facing each other could be likened to the Old Testament and the New Testament saints....
[48] Almost every Jewish commentator speaks of the threefold repetition of the word 'Holy' as a reference to the way God manifests His holiness 1) in heaven, 2) in this world, and 3) in the ages to come. Today we can see the Triune God being praised — Holy (Father), Holy, (Son), Holy (Spirit). Throughout church history this sacred chant was heard in liturgy, worship, and in song.

10

Filled with His Glory

"I am ruined!"

The world is a theater in which His perfect glory is displayed! Isaiah saw the sinfulness of man, the seraphim saw the glory of God. Isaiah had to see what the angels see. Every true voice for God must have the revelation of Glory filling the earth. Without this vision, we are only seeing part of the truth. What fills the earth is his glory, not our sinfulness. This is **Now**, not in the future. It is not, the whole earth 'will be' filled with His glory, we know that will come. It takes the vision of heaven to declare it today! We want to confine and restrict the glory, God fills the earth with it!

"At the sound of their voices the door posts and thresholds shook." A violent concussion hits like a bombshell … a tremendous shaking burst forth in the Temple of Holiness. Everything began to quake. Walls and posts and doors. Like Mt. Sinai trembling and shaking, so is the heavenly court as God's Holiness is seen and praised. No human voice or power could shake God's Temple, this was the celestial praises of God sung to their highest, that caused the Room to shake.

"And the temple was filled with smoke." [49] The glory cloud moved in and covered the entire scene. The fragrant incense of praise offered to God became a cloud of glory! This produced a solemn reverence and awe within Isaiah as he gazed on this incredible scene…. Isaiah is in the presence of the Lord Almighty, the Lord of Armies!

LIPS TOUCHED WITH FIRE! — 6:5–7

Isaiah saw the Lord Jesus (John 12:41). The prophet of God was taken into the Most Holy Place of the King's Throne Room, and there he witnessed the Holiness of The Most High. He overheard the burning seraphim chanting their chorus of praise. He smelled the Holy Smoke. He looked upon the Robe of Glory that surrounds Almighty God and the train of that Robe filled the Temple. The door posts and thresholds and pillars all quaked as Isaiah heard the words — **"The whole earth is filled with the glory of God."**

Isaiah's response to all this was pronouncing his 7th woe — **"Woe to me!"** No one comes before the holiness of God without devastation. Everything he boasted in was before his eyes as an abomination. What a shocking experience for God's prophet! It is the duty of a prophet to make declarations and announcements on God's behalf. Before honor could be given to Isaiah, he must be humbled and shattered by the revelation of the King … terror in the Temple!

Isaiah deserved what Uzziah received! Isaiah was one of the best of God's people — with anointed lips he had brought messages from God to the people. Yet he declares, **"I am ruined"** (Heb. 'finished, cut off, and pierced through, devastated, destroyed, doomed, undone and ruined'). He not only saw God, he saw Isaiah. One glimpse of God's holiness and he became a wretch in God's eyes. Our words are impure, our thoughts are crooked and hard, our heart is cold to the things of God — yet we do not see it until we see the One high and lifted up. There is something about this Throne Room revelation that forever changed the prophet Isaiah.

The Lord opened the heavens and he opened the prophet's eyes.... Until we have a vision of the Throne Room all we have to tell people is what is wrong with the world and what is wrong with them. Until we see from heaven's perspective all we have to preach is 'woe.' Vision brings hope. True vision brings true hope. We will never feed people from the Tree of Life, giving them the water from the satisfying River of God until we see the Lord high and lifted up. We must release hope, not woe. We must be filled with a vision of God's glory, not just man's sinfulness.

It is right to fear God and pronounce woe upon our flesh life. There is nothing in you or I to please God. Without Him we can do no good for He calls our righteousness, filthy rags. Our true nature is seen in the light of His piercing holiness. To see yourself as nothing, to humble yourself before God — that is good! Many in the church today will tell you its not needed, or don't go to far, or you will get over it. But God gives grace to the humble. It is because of our pride and arrogance that we don't see our need for God. We are unworthy servants — we are wise to humble our hearts in repentance.

We need to see Him as Isaiah did. When we do, we will no longer boast as though it depended on us. When we see the King, high and lifted up — we will cry out like Isaiah did. Most of us think revival is the roof blowing off, but in fact, it is the bottom falling out beneath the flesh of man. Woe to me! We lose all our confidence, our boasting is vain, our ways are crooked, our words are twisted, our motives are impure, our hearts are corrupt — Woe to me! I am ruined!

The parents of Samson had this experience.... *"We are doomed to die! ...We have seen God"* (Judges 13:22). Theirs was only an experience with the Angel of the Lord on earth ... Isaiah saw the glorified Son of God with His Royal Robes! Daniel had a similar experience with an angel that touched his lips (Dan.10)! The Lord reached out His hand and touched the mouth of Jeremiah. This enabled the prophet to speak the words of God (Jer.1:9 & Isa.51:16).

Job had heard with of God's majesty but when his eyes saw the whirlwind of God — *"Therefore I despise myself and repent in dust and ashes* (42:5–6)." Peter said, Go away from Lord, for I am a sinful man. Paul was blinded for three days until Ananias came with the healing word, John fell at His feet as though he were dead — everyone who came into the manifest presence of the Lord was devastated!

"A man — unclean of lips am I!" The seraphs could praise the Lord with pure lips, but not Isaiah. His lips were unclean, which means his heart and life were unclean. Isaiah could not praise the holiness of God like the seraphim!

Isaiah was a prophet who made his living from speaking. Yet he calls himself a man with unclean lips. He declares himself a sinner who has offended with his words. He has offended others, and he has offended the holiness of God. Polluted with sin, his words, like ours, are "unclean" ('foul, defiled, polluted, contaminated').

"My eyes have seen the King!" Isaiah heard the holy angels singing of the holiness of God and he realized his lips were not holy — he was ruined by the revelation of the **King**! The majesty of this King left him undone and shattered! When you see God seated on the throne all you can think about is your uncleanness. Who shall ascend the Hill of the Lord and stand in His Holy Place? Not Isaiah ... nor you or I. Only the One who had clean hands and a pure heart — Jesus Christ!

BURNING ONES! — 6:6–7

"Then one of the seraphs[50] flew to me with a live coal in his hand, which he had taken with tongs from the altar." Instead of ushering Isaiah out of the Holy Place and throwing him out on his ear, a provision was made for his cleansing. Judgment upon sin from the Most Holy Place is far different from man's view (6 woes) outside. Isaiah only could speak woe — he could show the nation what was wrong ... but until he went into the Holy Place he had no answers. God will deal with uncleanness **In Grace.** He will release the purging fire to remove guilt.

Isaiah's vision of the Lord was full of glory and grace. The majesty of the Lord was lifted high, but so was His tender mercy to provide cleansing for the sinner. His grace is as remarkable as His glory! In answer to his cry, Isaiah's sin was purged and removed. All of this is an unveiling of the wonderful reality of the kindness of God.... The One who receives the worship of seraphim also will hear the words of a sinner who cries out to Him.

One of the burning ones took a live coal (from the same word as seraphim) and brought it to Isaiah. Purging and cleansing only comes to the humble soul. Visions of glory will turn to visits of grace. God's prophet was cleansed by the burning coal.... Isaiah prophesied in Chapter 4 that God would cleanse guilt with the spirit of judgment and a spirit of fire! Now he experiences this firsthand.

Burning in the presence of the Lord is an altar of incense that burns continually. It is an emblem of the cross and what the Son of God would do to be consumed as God's sacrifice and be a sweet smelling fragrance of life to God. This altar of incense speaks of the satisfaction God has with the work of His Son. Nothing will cleanse our lives like the fire of the Cross. When God judged sin, only coals of fire were left — it speaks of a finished sacrifice.

Before that same altar of incense Uzziah once stood in presumption … now Isaiah stands in the discovery of his own unworthiness. Isaiah saw firsthand that the holiness that made Isaiah a leper can kill and maim … but Isaiah will see firsthand that this holiness can also cleanse and forgive.

The cross is the live coal that touches our lips in purging fire. Jesus became the sacrifice that endured the judgment of God for our sins. Do you know what it takes to have your sin purged? Jesus was beaten and crucified; we are left with blistered lips by a coal of fire. Our lips are tender; this is why we express our tenderness with another by our lips. Can you feel a burning coal of fire sizzling on your lips?

The word for coal is 'ritzpah'[51] and means ceremonial stone. Upon the 'ritzpah' stone was poured the incense and then the stone was placed in the fire creating the fragrance of the burning sacrifice of the Lamb of God. This white-hot stone was placed on Isaiah's lips — could this be the "white stone" of Revelation 2:17?

WHO WILL GO FOR US? — 6:8–10

Who will go for the cause of heaven? Many will go for recognition or for a paycheck, but who are those who will go only for the heaven's fame? Are you ready to say to God, **"Here am I send me."** But you are woeful and ruined with lips that are unclean…. How could you go? How could you be the one He sends? Grace and cleansing is the answer! The only way a man is fit to serve is when he has been cleansed by the coal of fire. A purged and cleansed vessel. God has requirements to fulfill before He sends you forth....

7 Requirements of the Divine Call:

1. **Revelation of *God,* high and lifted up. (v 1–4)**
2. **A revelation of *Holiness.* (v 1–4)**
3. **A revelation of our *Uncleanness* (v 5)**
4. **Divine cleansing. (v 6–7)**
5. **A personal call — the voice of the Lord. (v 8)**
6. **Abandonment to God. (v 8)**
7. **Divine commissioning. (v 9–13)**

The first five chapters of Isaiah are the judgments of God upon sin as it is seen in the outer court ... Isaiah 6 is what judgment upon sin looks like when you stand in the Holy Place! This vision will change you forever, even as it changed the ministry of Isaiah. His words from this point on go deeper, linger longer, and speak more clearly of the heart of the God who cleanses by fire. Isaiah must learn to speak the powerful word of God that creates and transforms the earth; this is why he must be sent with cleansed lips.

ISAIAH'S MISSION — 6:10–13

"Go and tell this people: "'Be ever hearing, but never understanding; be ever seeing, but never perceiving.' Make the heart of this people calloused; make their ears dull and close their eyes. Otherwise they might see with their eyes, hear with their ears, understand with their hearts, and turn and be healed."

Isaiah saw the Lord and was sent to men. With fire-touched lips Isaiah was told to make the blind, blinder and the deaf, deafer. Isaiah was sent not in triumph but in testing. Not to be admired and loved, but despised and rejected ... and eventually to be sawn in half.

The first effect of Isaiah's throne room anointing and newly given prophetic task would be to increase the blindness and insensitivity of God's people. But isn't the purpose of the Word of God to open the blind eyes and bring understanding to the heart? Yes, but only if the heart is tender and right with God.

The task of the prophet is not merely to open the eyes, but to blind the eyes of the rebellious and vindicate God's character in sending His judgments. Preaching truth is not merely to meet man's need but to meet God's need. The Lord has a need to touch a prophet with a coal of fire and send him forth to preach in order to vindicate God. The Lord was to be great in eyes and justified in all He does. We go and speak to satisfy God's heart, not just those who hear us.

This is the strangest commission ever given to a prophet. 'Go tell the truth … and tell them they will not understand. Bring a hardening of their hearts with your message, Isaiah. Release a spiritual blindness upon them so they will hear and be converted!'

Isaiah was commissioned to have an unsuccessful ministry. The prophet's voice makes them blinder, deader, duller, and darkened even more. Yet, Isaiah was sent to highlight the guilt of a nation. He will be confronting a total inability to comprehend his message. Isaiah would be anointed and with a clear message, but eyes would be closed to see the truth and be transformed. Some people believe they are sophisticated and ready to hear the word of the Lord … but few are prepared for authentic prophetic proclamation.

The effect of truth is often to irritate stubborn hearts. Truth can even make men more wicked, yet the prophet's task is to proclaim it regardless. The response of the people can never alter or soften the words God gives us to speak. It is not merely the truth God wants people to know…. He wants them to know their own hearts in light of the truth. Throne room prophets are about to be released to the earth!

To those who have an ear for God and a heart to receive revelation, more will be given. To those who do not have a heart to heart God, even the little revelation they have will be taken from them (Matt.13:11–15). This is why Jesus came speaking in parables. He longed for the open heart to receive more and the closed heart would be blinded further. **"Calloused"** hearts can never receive the ways of God.

The prophet's dilemma is this: If the people don't hear your message, your only recourse is to make it plainer and more pointed. But to do this exposes them to a greater risk of rejecting a greater light.

Light rejected hardens the heart. Eventually, they will harden beyond recovery, calloused in sin. Verses 9–10 are so important that they are quoted six times in the New Testament (Matt.13:13–15; Mark 4:12; Luke 8:10; John 12:40; Acts 28:25–28; Rom.11:8). God does not deliberately make sinners blind, deaf, and hard-hearted; but the more that people resist God's truth; the less able they are to receive God's truth. But the servant is to proclaim the Word no matter how people respond, for the test of ministry is not outward success but faithfulness to the Lord.

THE HOLY SEED — 6:11-13

"Then I said, "For how long, O Lord?" And he answered: "Until the cities lie ruined and without inhabitant, until the houses are left deserted and the fields ruined and ravaged, until the *Lord* has sent everyone far away and the land is utterly forsaken. And though a tenth remains in the land, it will again be laid waste. But as the terebinth and oak leave stumps when they are cut down, so the holy seed will be the stump in the land."

Out of love and compassion for his people, Isaiah asks God — 'How long is my commission to remain in force?' God's reply: Until the desired end was reached: cities would be ruined, houses deserted, fields ravaged and captives taken to a land far away. Then they would be ready to listen. As Isaiah preached the hearts would grow harder, more closed, more calloused. This would continue until God's people would be taken captive. Notice the prophet doesn't ask God to modify His declaration; Isaiah knows the people are to be taken captive.

[The anointing of God will one day capture cities with the gospel, leaving the houses of dead religion empty, laying waste the fields of this world by the Word of His mouth. A great revival will one day take away the lost into the captivity of hope and love!]

This is not the end, but a new beginning. God will not do away with His people, for His people are His plan. Just as Isaiah could stand in the presence of the burning ones and not be destroyed, so God's people even in a time of judgment will not be forsaken. Forgiveness will be extended by the grace of the Bridegroom God... and a fresh beginning will come. Isaiah received a new beginning, and so will his people. He has now become a prophet of hope, even in a time of desolation.

God removes the first to establish the second. The sons of Noah were the **"holy seed"** of a new beginning of the human race. When a tree is cut down there is a still life in the tree. A new Judah will arise, a people of praise that will release the next stage of God's process of mingling Himself with man ... the Holy Seed will come forth one day. True believers are the 'holy seed'[52] for they have been born from above. With the very DNA of God they carry His life, His genes. As seed, we can give life to others as God places us in the ground to die and multiply....

The seed of the kingdom is the word of God bursting forth in the human heart (Mark 4).

[49] Smoke is mentioned seven times in Isaiah — 4:5, 6:4, 9:18, 14:31, 34:10, 51:6, 65:5.
[50] This word means 'fiery ones' or 'burning ones', as is supposed, to their burning love. They are represented as "standing" above the King as he sat upon his throne, ready at once to minister unto him. Their form appears to have been human, with the addition of wings.
[51] The Hebrew word 'ritzpah' is taken from the same root word as 'seraphim' and can also mean — 'lightning , hot thunderbolt, burning coal.'
[52] Or, 'the seed of holiness its stump.' Isaiah uses the word 'seed' 25 times in his writings. "These stumps are the sacred race...." Moffat Translation

11

The Book of Immanuel

"Be careful, keep calm and don't be afraid."

The ancient title given to chapters 7–12 is: The Book of Immanuel. This section of "the vision" (1:1) contains incredible revelation about how God would come to earth and branch out through redeemed human beings. God is the Vine, His people will become branches. A new nature is about to be planted in the soil of humanity. Broken stumps will not keep God from bursting forth in the human spirit with power and virtue. Immanuel is a term used for this new creation life coming down out of heaven. It will begin as a **Man**, but will soon become **Men/ Women**. Immanuel is the partnership of heaven and earth, God and humanity.

THE WASHERMAN'S FIELD — 7:1–6

"When Ahaz son of Jotham, the son of Uzziah, was king of Judah, King Rezin[53] of Aram and Pekah[54] son of Remaliah king of Israel marched up to fight against Jerusalem, but they could not overpower it. Now the house of David[55] was told, "Aram has allied itself with Ephraim"; so the hearts of Ahaz and his people were shaken, as the trees of the forest are shaken by the wind."

Judah is being threatened. An unholy alliance has formed to invade if King Ahaz will not agree to surrender. Isaiah's prophetic message for Judah was not a military strategy, but a strong message of faith in God. It can never be a matter of military muscle or clever strategies, but the passion to trust God to win every battle. The moment of decision had come for Judah, to enter into alliances or to enter into the realm of faith.

Two kings, two principalities rose up against the king of Judah, Ahaz. Threatened by those around him, Ahaz was a frightened man. Ephraim and Syria joined each other to overthrow Ahaz and put **"the son of Tabeel"** on the throne in his place. The pressure was on the king, Ahaz, to join this united front against the Assyrian expansion.

The wind has come to shake the "trees of the forest." But there is a Tree where we hide and find shelter. This was the Tree Ahaz (and you and I) must discover). In Christ, we will not be moved by the winds of adversity.

"Then the LORD said to Isaiah, "Go out, you and your son Shear-Jashub[56], to meet Ahaz at the end of the aqueduct of the Upper Pool, on the road to the Washerman's Field. Say to him, 'Be careful, keep calm and don't be afraid. Do not lose heart because of these two smoldering stubs of firewood — because of the fierce anger of Rezin and Aram and of the son of Remaliah. Aram, Ephraim and Remaliah's son have plotted your ruin, saying, "Let us invade Judah; let us tear it apart and divide it among ourselves, and make the son of Tabeel king over it."

Isaiah had asked to be sent; now God instructs him to **"Go."** Isaiah's son was named Shear-Jashub, "a remnant shall return." Isaiah's little boy carried a sermon in his name. This son becomes a living oracle, a visual aid of what God had planned to do. Shear-Jashub literally becomes the word made flesh. Judgment was coming but a remnant will not be destroyed but will return to their place of blessing and inheritance. Isaiah's son is a message of grace.

The Lord commanded Isaiah to take his son Shear-Jashub, and meet Ahaz as the king was inspecting the city's water system. The **"aqueduct of the Upper Pool"** was also part of the city's defenses, built in preparation of the coming siege. Jerusalem's water supply was above ground and vulnerable. It is when we are vulnerable that we are on the road to being purified and made ready for God to use — the **"road to the Washerman's Field."** The heavenly *Washerman* wants to cleanse our hearts from unbelief, hiding in false belief systems, and closing our heart from a true work of the Spirit. God wants to make you an 'aqueduct' or channel of the Upper (heavenly) Pool!

Ahaz's faith had been wavering, and the hearts of his people had been shaking for fear (Isa. 7:2); but Isaiah came with a message of assurance: **"Be careful, keep calm, don't be afraid."** Such wise counsel when we feel surrounded. How would Ahaz find this inner peace? By believing God's promise that Judah's enemies would be defeated. "Do not lose heart" (courage). Faith in God's promises is the only way to find peace in the midst of trouble. *"You will keep him in perfect peace, whose mind is stayed on You, because he trusts in You"* (26:3, NKJV).

Aram and Ephraim were described as "smoldering stubs." Their combined might could not stand up against the Assyrian invasion. Why would Ahaz fear them? Will Ahaz trust in politics or promises? Will it be an alliance of forces or an advance of faith? Their fire was spent, nothing was left within them. Why would you or I trust in our flesh or in our intellect? They cannot help in a day of trouble.

Why would we fear our enemies? All our foes are nothing compared to the promises of certain victory in Jesus Christ our Lord.

STAND FIRM — 7:7–9

"Yet this is what the Sovereign Lord says: "'It will not take place, it will not happen, for the head of Aram is Damascus, and the head of Damascus is only Rezin. Within sixty-five years Ephraim will be too shattered to be a people. The head of Ephraim is Samaria, and the head of Samaria is only Remaliah's son. If you do not stand firm in your faith, you will not stand at all.'"

Within sixty-five years, Ephraim (Israel, the Northern Kingdom) would be gone forever. Isaiah spoke this prophecy in the year 734 B.C. Assyria defeated Syria in 732 B.C. and invaded Israel in 722 B.C. They deported many of the Jews and assimilated the rest by introducing Gentiles into the land; and by 669 B.C. (sixty-five years later), the nation no longer existed. God's Word is always true.

Notice that the "head" of a nation was a city and the "head" of a city was a man. This is the principle of the stronghold/strongman. If the chief city of a nation is taken, the nation will fall. If the chief man/spirit in a city is taken, then the city will fall.

But Ahaz was instructed to mix faith with the prophetic promises Isaiah delivered. We must be willing to take God at His word and lay our fears to rest, or we will be insecure, unstable, and unable to stand against the foe.

A SIGN FROM GOD — 7:10–14

"Again the Lord spoke to Ahaz, "Ask the Lord your God for a sign, whether in the deepest depths or in the highest heights." But Ahaz said, "I will not ask; I will not put the Lord to the test." Then Isaiah said, "Hear now, you house of David! Is it not enough to try the patience of men? Will you try the patience of my God also?"

God knows our weakness and our unbelief and is committed to convince us that His power is real. So Isaiah brings the word from God to Ahaz: 'Go ahead, ask Me for a sign and make it big, make it something impossible to man. For I always work in human impossibilities.' Realizing the weakness of the king's faith, Isaiah offered to give a sign to encourage him; but Ahaz put on a "pious front" and rudely refused his offer. Knowing that he was secretly allied with Assyria, how could Ahaz honestly ask the Lord for a special sign? So, instead of speaking only to the king, Isaiah addressed the whole "house of David" and gave the prophecy concerning "Immanuel."

"Therefore the LORD himself will give you a sign[57]: The virgin will be with child and will give birth to a son, and will call him Immanuel."

The greatest sign or proof that God could give us is to become a Man. By joining Himself (His life and nature) to the human properties, is a sign that startles us all. Jesus is the virgin-born Son of God. He has become the Son of Man. Nothing in all of eternity can be compared to this. The Creator lays aside the outward glory and takes up the nature and body of a human being. God in our nature. The 'with-us' God!

This "Immanuel" prophecy has both an immediate and a future fulfillment. By the time the child is grown up, the enemies of Judah shall have been destroyed. **And** the True Immanuel will come one day and be the greatest Sign God has ever given to mankind. The Hebrew makes it clear, '**The** virgin' will conceive. It is nothing less than the Immaculate Conception, the virgin-birth of the God-Man.

The *ultimate* fulfillment of this prophecy is in our Lord Jesus Christ, who is "God with us" (Matt. 1:18–25; Luke 1:31–35). The virgin birth of Christ is a key doctrine; for if Jesus Christ is not God come in sinless human flesh, then we have no Savior. Jesus had to be born of a virgin, apart from human generation, because

He existed before His mother. He was not just born in this world; He came down from heaven *into* the world (John 3:13; 6:33, 38, 41–42, 50–51, 58). Jesus was *sent by the Father* and therefore came into the world having a human mother but not a human father (4:34; 5:23–24, 30; 9:4).

However, this "sign" had an *immediate* significance to Ahaz and the people of Judah. A woman who was then a virgin would get married, conceive, and bear a son whose name would be "Immanuel." This son would be a reminder that God was with His people and would care for them. It is likely that this virgin was Isaiah's second wife, his first wife having died after Shear-Jashub was born; and that Isaiah's second son was named both "Immanuel" and "Maher-shalal-hash-baz."

DIET OF THE KINGDOM — 7:15–16

"He will eat curds and honey when he knows enough to reject the wrong and choose the right. But before the boy knows enough to reject the wrong and choose the right, the land of the two kings you dread will be laid waste."

This coming Son will be one who has the kingdom promises as His diet. Milk and honey speak of the promised land, where all God's promises are fulfilled. Jesus is the only One who has fulfilled the Father's desires. Feeding on the promises enabled Him to choose the right. He resisted temptation by the Word of God dwelling in Him. Strength to reject evil comes from feeding on truth.

This is also a prophecy that the land would soon be laid waste by the confederate powers of Israel and Syria before Isaiah's child was weaned from the breast.

THE WHISTLER — 8:17–19

"The Lord will bring on you and on your people and on the house of your father a time unlike any since Ephraim broke away from

Judah — he will bring the king of Assyria. In that day the Lord will whistle for flies from the distant streams of Egypt and for bees from the land of Assyria. They will all come and settle in the steep ravines and in the crevices in the rocks, on all the thorn bushes and at all the water holes."

Isaiah prophesies the coming judgment. The Lord will **"whistle"** and attract the demonic powers associated with Egypt into the land. God will summons the army to come and execute His decreed purpose.

Experts tell us that beekeepers can persuade bees to come out of their hives or return from the fields by whistling. Like bees gathering to sting, these warriors will assemble into every compromise.

The **"steep ravines"** are a picture of the slippery slopes of darkness that bring defeat into our hearts. These "flies" and bees are found where there is corruption and decay. Our fallen hearts quickly become the gathering place of demonic powers. **"Crevices in the rocks"** speak of our hidden compromises. The **"thorn bushes"** are symbols of our flesh life with its briars and offences that does not yield to God. The **"water holes"** point us to the stagnating places in our spirit that we have not allowed to be renewed and revived.

THE LORD'S RAZOR — 8:20–22

"In that day the Lord will use a razor hired from beyond the River — the king of Assyria — to shave your head and the hair of your legs, and to take off your beards also. In that day, a man will keep alive a young cow and two goats. And because of the abundance of the milk they give, he will have curds to eat. All who remain in the land will eat curds and honey."

The next image the Lord uses to show His power is that of a "razor." This supernatural 'shaver' will be Assyria coming to cut off their pride, their glory, and their boast. Often the victors would shave the heads of the vanquished. Mourners had their heads shaved (Isaiah 15:12) so Judah will mourn over their ways as judgment falls. The beauty of the land will be cut off and destroyed by the razor of the Lord.

1000 VINES, 1000 SHEKELS — 8:23–25

In that day, in every place where there were a thousand vines worth a thousand silver shekels, there will be only briers and thorns. Men will go there with bow and arrow, for the land will be covered with briers and thorns. As for all the hills once cultivated by the hoe, you will no longer go there for fear of the briers and thorns; they will become places where cattle are turned loose and where sheep run."

Where there once was produce and fruit, there will remain only briars and thorns — so complete will be the stripping of the land. Valuable, precious land that could sustain 1000 vines would be devastated by the swarming armies of Assyria.

The 1000 vines and 1000 shekels are also mentioned in Song of Songs 8:11–12, *"Solomon had a vineyard in Baal Hamon; he let out his vineyard to tenants. Each was to bring for its fruit a thousand shekels of silver. But my own vineyard is mine to give; the thousand shekels are for you, O Solomon, and two hundred are for those who tend its fruit."*

This parable shows us the value of our Bridegroom's love. The number 1000 speaks of fullness of maturity and worth. Christ's love for us can be compared to the value of over 5 pounds of silver (redeeming love).

[53] His name means, 'wicked pleasure' — a picture of the life of the flesh.
[54] Pekah means, 'open-eyed, seeing' — a picture of human reasoning.
[55] The "house of David" is used here for the king himself. Ahaz is the personification of the royal family of David.
[56] The names of three sons are given in Chapters 7–8, Shear-Jasub (7:1–9), Immanuel (7:10–17), and Maher-Shalal-Haz-Baz (8:1–4). It is likely that all three were the sons of Isaiah. They each speak of **Hope**.
[57] The Hebrew is plural. A double sign!

12

OUR SANCTUARY

"THE LORD SPOKE ... WITH
HIS STRONG HAND UPON ME."

God is going to supernaturally and sovereignly introduce this generation to the anointing of the prophets. The Old Testament prophets spoke the oracles of God. Their lives were messages and their messages brought life. It is crucial that the saints of the last days walk in the same authority and power as the prophets of old. Isaiah's mantle is available again for those who will go into the throne zone and receive the coal of fire. The Spirit of Elijah is releasing the anointing of the Prophets. Listen to the words God gave to Isaiah:

"The Lord said to me, "Take a large scroll and write on it with an ordinary pen: Maher-Shalal-Hash-Baz. And I will call in Uriah

the priest and Zechariah son of Jeberekiah as reliable witnesses for me." Then I went to the prophetess, and she conceived and gave birth to a son. And the Lord said to me, "Name him Maher-Shalal-Hash-Baz. Before the boy knows how to say 'My father' or 'My mother,' the wealth of Damascus and the plunder of Samaria will be carried off by the king of Assyria."

Isaiah was instructed by God to write on a large scroll the name of his yet to be born son, Maher-Shalal-Hash-Baz. This was to be witnessed by two reliable men, Uriah the priest and Zechariah. The Lord wants to validate His Word. More than once God instructs His prophets to write out the Word of the Lord (Hab.2:2). We are to make it plain, clear and understood by others.

"With an ordinary pen" God can use what is written by man to touch man. Weak, frail man has the grace to write and speak and pray.... It was with the *hand of a man* that God wrote on the wall for Belshazzar and all his guests to see.

Isaiah then goes to his wife, who was a prophetess and they have the child. What a prophetic couple. Together they would minister the Word of the Lord. God anointed the prophetess as well as the prophet. She would literally give birth to the Word of God! She is a type of the Virgin Mary, who prophesied over her son, giving birth to the incarnate Logos of God.

At the birth of their son, God spoke again and told them the symbolic name of the child, which would be a sign of the coming invasion of the Assyrian armies. Isaiah's scroll would have this as its title: Maher-Shalal-Hash-Baz. The two witnesses would verify what God had spoken to Isaiah, before it came to pass. Perhaps this scroll was unfurled like a banner outside Isaiah's house ... or placed over the gateway into the Temple area. It would have been publicized in some visible fashion. Some translate the word scroll as 'tablet' (writing board or placard). This yet to be born son was to be named Maher-Shalal-Hash-Baz, which means 'quick to the plunder, swift to the spoil.' This would mean the invading armies would not consider the battle, only the spoil that awaits them. With zeal and fervor they will conquer everything in their path.

As the people would pass by this sign they would wonder ... what does it mean. This was a vivid way to make know the prophecy. God has creative ways to get His Word out to the people. Before this prophetic child was old enough to talk, the prophecy was fulfilled: Assyria plundered Damascus and Samaria.

We must remember, Judah was confronted by a coalition of made up of Israel's ten northern tribes (worldly, carnal church) and Syria (unbelievers) who wanted what Judah had. They wanted Jerusalem, its wealth and blessings. Others always want the spiritual blessings of God but don't want to pay the price to get them. Isaiah had told Judah not to panic over Israel and Syria coming against them. God would send another nation, Assyria who would come and destroy first Syria then Israel (Samaria), after which they would come against Jerusalem.

GENTLY FLOWING OR MIGHTY FLOODWATERS? — 8:5–8

"The Lord spoke to me again: Because this people has rejected the gently flowing waters of Shiloah and rejoices over Rezin and Remaliah, therefore the Lord is about to bring against them the mighty floodwaters of the River — the king of Assyria...."

The prophet Isaiah receives another word.... The Lord shows him that judgment from Assyria is coming to the land because they had rejected the gently flowing waters of Shiloah. This was a spring of water that is known today as 'En sitti Miryam.' Historians tell us it was a canal or spring of water that flowed underneath the Temple area. Worshippers could be refreshed from its pleasant stream and the water would be used for sacred purposes in the Temple worship. It was later channeled by Hezekiah into a pool called the pool of Siloam.

This stream originated in Gihon ... it is a picture of the Davidic monarchy, the kingdom of David, which passed to his son, Solomon. This transfer of power was done at Gihon (I Kings 1:33–34). And it is a picture of Jerusalem with the refreshing of God's presence within her walls. Here is the figure of speech that Isaiah is presenting:

'Since you have rejected the trickle of Shiloah, the rivers that flow by the House of God, the gentle rule of God's kingdom ... you will be conquered by the kingdom of a tyrant from Assyria (Tiglath-Pileazer). Since, you have rejoiced in a military alliance with other nations and make their leadership your boast — you will be conquered by another nation who will overwhelm you and take you up to your neck in despair. Your king (Ahaz) and your city will reap the devastating consequences of abandoning the Lord. Because you rejected peace (Shiloah) you will taste war.'

Shiloah represents a relationship God sought to have with His people. He longed to be their fountain and their peace Flowing within them as a gentle stream. Instead they rejected this relationship and sought their peace and comfort in a military alliance with Syria and Israel. The disobedient nation will be inundated with the floodwaters of Assyrian armies, even up to their necks. They must sink or swim, for the flood will reach to their necks. Still the Lord holds out a promise to preserve those who walk in the fear of God.

- ➢ The River = the Euphrates River in Assyria
- ➢ Shiloah = peace
- ➢ Euphrates = floodwaters

When you choose the world, you will be overwhelmed by the world. If we reject the stream of refreshing leadership under the Holy Spirit and refuse to dwell in His sweet presence, we can expect to be devoured by the world. The key to purity is the gentle stream of Shiloah ... underground springs that supply our true life.

"Its outspread wings" is a picture of the armies will cover the land. Help us O, Immanuel! This is intercession for the Savior to come and rescue the land.

God Is With Us! — 8:9–12

"Raise the war cry, you nations, and be shattered! Listen, all you distant lands. Prepare for battle, and be shattered! Prepare for battle, and be shattered! Devise your strategy, but it will be thwarted; propose your plan, but it will not stand, for God is with us!"

This is the truth of Psalm 2! God laughs at the plans of the nations ... they will come to nothing. Their plans will fall back upon them and shatter them to pieces. For **"Immanuel!"** The security of His Name!

God is with us, and if God be for us who can be against us! Because of the prophetic purposes of God, the schemes of the nations will be thwarted. All their alliances, their hostile plans will be without success.

"The Lord spoke to me with His strong hand upon me, warning me not to follow the way of this people." This was a divine revelation that came to Isaiah. It came with the strong hand of God upon him. He was seized by God — a compelling, gripping power fell upon Isaiah as he prophesied this word that came to him. It will take the strong hand of God on your life to keep you free from the world and the tug of the flesh. Only the hand of God can deliver us from our fears and keep us walking in the awe of God.

It is time to distance yourself from this people.... **"Do not call conspiracy everything that these people call conspiracy; do not fear what they fear, and do not dread it." Or** 'Do not seek a confederacy (alliance) every time these people call for a confederacy (alliance).' Don't join with the world that just thinks numbers means power and success. Fear is what drives them on. Do not fear the things they are panicking over. Don't fear the phantom menace. I Pet.3:14

SANCTUARY OR SNARE? — 8:13–15

"The Lord Almighty is the One you are to regard as holy, He is the One you are to fear, He is the One you are to dread." What is the fear of God? The Hebrew word for **Fear** means holy awe, to venerate, deepest respect, worship, adore, to regard as holy. Is the fear of God firmly planted in your heart? Are you defiled by the world? Going after both God and selfish pleasures? Let Him be the One you fear! Let Him inspire you with awe! Set Him apart in your heart as Holy!

Don't confuse a *"spirit of fear"* with the **Fear Of The Lord**. God does not give us a spirit of fear or panic, but He does insist we approach Him with a circumcised heart, with reverence, awe, humility, and surrender. We have always known that **Love** is the foundation of our relationship with God, but now the Lord wants us to discover the fear of the Lord as equally foundational. John says God is **Love** but before this, he taught us God is **Light** (Holy). Love and the Fear of God are the twin truths that stabilize the church. To emphasize one without the other is error. Paul wrote — *"knowing therefore the terror of the LORD, we persuade men."* And in the same chapter he wrote — *"the love of Christ compels us to give our all to Him."* (2 Cor.5:11–14)

The Holy Fear of God is the key to knowing Him as He yearns to be known. Lev.9:22–10:3 and Prov.3:7–8 *"Do not be wise in your own eyes; fear the LORD and shun evil. This will bring health to your body and nourishment to your bones."*

Do you think the Lord of Lords is going to come to a place where He is not given the reverence due Him? What if every time you went to visit your friend's house, they answered the door with "O, its you again … come on in." What kind of welcome would that be? You wouldn't be too keen on visiting them again would you. How do we view the Lord? How high of a place have we given Him? Do we honor Him, or give Him the leftovers? Whenever we come together we need to **Honor His Name And His Word!** Ps.34:9 Fear the Lord you His saints, for those who fear Him lack nothing.

Irreverence leads to rebellion, presumption and arrogance. God is about to flatten the pride of man. The Spirit of Elijah is in the land … the spirit of burning will cleanse the filth of the daughters of Zion. Refiner's fire will burn up the dross of the uncrucified flesh life of every one of us. We will no longer defend ourselves and hide behind a shallow repentance. Our hollow hearts will be exposed. Light will pierce us — true brokenness of heart and a contrite spirit will distinguish us from those vain boasters of this world.

We are about to see what angels see — Holy, Holy, Holy is their cry. You will not be admitted into the presence of the King without the fear of God. II Cor.7:1, Heb.12:25–29, Phil.2:12, Ps.5:7, I Pet.1:13– 2:8

If you make **Him** your fear, you will find Him as your hope and rest. "He will be a Sanctuary." Our God is a Sanctuary in the midst of turmoil. He is our **Holy Place** of rest. He is coming to dwell with His people. You are defended and secure in Him when He is your dread. All around you will be a wall of holiness and quietness to shield your heart from fear.... He will be like Temple walls all about you. He will be your Sanctification — I Cor.1:30.

For the believer, this Holy Sanctuary will be our hope, but for the unbeliever His dwelling among us will be **"a stone that causes men to stumble and a rock that makes them fall."** To one He is peace, to another doom. Because they ignore Him, they trip over Him — the Rock of stumbling causes them to fall from their place of self-confidence and arrogant boasting. Ps.91:12, Jer.6:19–21, Ezek.3:19

Jesus Himself is glorious and a Friend of sinners. The cause of the stumbling is that they resist Him. They trip over Him and fall into sins that drown the soul. The cause is not an angry Jesus but a rebellious heart that is opened to darkness because of rejection of the Light. Its like, God puts a rock in front of them to slow them down, to make them stop and think. Instead of seeing that Rock as the mercy of God wanting to save their soul, they trip over Him and fall into even greater darkness. To refuse God's warning is to stumble to your death.

"A trap and a snare" — To those who are hostile to the King. The **Holiness** of God is a great stumbling block and offence to the unsaved. The **Holiness** of God is the greatest danger to the unsaved. This **Holy** God is both a Sanctuary and a Snare — depending on how people respond to His holiness. God's judgment catches the world by surprise; like a trap closing suddenly. God's holiness will be a springing trap to the unsaved; no one will escape.

Peter reflects on this passage in Isaiah and says this.... "*A Stone that causes men to stumble and a Rock that makes them fall. They stumble because they disobey the message — which is what they were destined for.*" I Pet.2:8 You cannot make the Bible completely clear to everybody. There are those who will not hear no matter how clear you present truth. It is the will of the heart that is the doorway to truth. Not the intellect, but the will. God makes it clear to the willing heart!

TRUSTING THE HIDDEN GOD — 8:16–17

"Bind up the testimony and seal up the law among my disciples." God tells Isaiah to simply leave it at that — there is nothing else he could do that to impart this revelation to the disciples of the Lord. Only those with a heart to know the truth will receive it. Disciples mean 'instructed or trained ones' — those who are being taught by the Lord (Isa.50:4, 54:13). They are God's disciples, not Isaiah's.

Every time we preach and teach the truths of God, we are sealing up His testimony in the hearts of men. This is the work of every faithful proclaimer of truth — we are expressing God's testimony to the hearts of others. The revelation of judgment to come is a testimony from God that is to be bound up in our hearts.

So that when we witness devastation, we can have a measure of understanding and a buffer in our hearts protecting us from accusing God of being unmerciful.

"Bind up" means to wrap around (safeguarding it from tampering). **"Seal up"** means to declare it final and unchanging. *Perhaps this could be compared to a Notary Public verifying to the nation that Isaiah told them ahead of time.*

"I will wait for the Lord who is hiding His face from the house of Jacob. I will put my trust in Him." Faith and confidence enables us to wait for the Lord to act. God will fulfill His Word; the word of His prophets will come to pass. Even when God hides His face, faith endures. **Faith** is for the dark day. True faith is designed to be your strength when God seems absent.

God's judgment is a time of hiding His face from the people of the earth. To the "disciples" of the Lord, it is a time to make **Him** our dread and our fear — hiding in our knowledge of His love as our Sanctuary. Peace in a time of judgment comes from knowing that God is good and kind. Bind this testimony into your heart. The Lord **"hiding His face"** is the opposite of *"the LORD making His face to shine"* (lifting up the light of His countenance). Instead of an approachable God, those on the earth will find a season when the face of the Lord is hidden. Can we wait in confidence and put our trust in Him even when we don't feel Him near?

CHILDREN ARE FOR SIGNS & WONDERS! — 8:18

"Here am I and the children the Lord has given me. We are signs and symbols in Israel from the Lord Almighty, who dwells on Mount Zion." This verse has a dual meaning. Obviously, it speak of Isaiah and his sons. Isaiah's name is a prophecy of what God wants to be to His people — 'Jehovah saves.' His first son was named Shear Jashub — 'a remnant will return.' And his second son's name Maher-Shalal-Hash-Baz is a prophecy of what is about to take place. "Quick to the plunder, swift to the spoil" is exactly what will happen as the Assyrian army overruns the land. So Isaiah and his sons are prophetic signposts to the nation of what God wants to tell them; tokens of future events. But there is yet another meaning to all this....

Isaiah is a type or picture of Christ that would come to the earth (Immanuel). In Hebrews 2:13 this verse is quoted in reference to the Lord Jesus Christ. This is a prophecy of the coming harvest! After the fires of judgment subside, there will be an ingathering of souls and Jesus will cause them to be signs and wonders to the whole earth! Christ and His disciples (sons) will be for signs and wonders (miracles). The Lord of Hosts (lit, 'the Lord of armies') dwells on Mt. Zion. A spiritual picture of God's people; Mt. Zion is not just a place but a realm where God and His people walk in fellowship together. God wants to dwell with those consecrated ones (Isa.50:5) that have entered into covenant with sacrifice.

NO LIGHT OF DAWN — 8:19–22

This is the voice of Messiah speaking to His people — warning them not to turn to counterfeit voices that will lead His people astray. There is no New Age channel that can give us more than the pure Word of the Lord. He alone can foretell the future and guide our lives.

God's people had turned to mediums and wizards and they begin to seek the dead. People are crying out for revelation: 'Give me illumination. I want an experience of the supernatural. I'm not seeing the signs and wonders in the church today, so I'll call up the psychic hotline.' It's what's happening in the church today.

When we don't have signs and wonders, the world goes off and looks for it in another place. They look for it in the new age and the occult and the false expressions of genuine revelation. God wants us to have it in the church today so the world can know there's revelation and understanding in the church. They should be saying, 'I'm not even a Christian, but they knew something about my uncle and they knew something about the sickness in my body and they knew something about my younger brother and that tells me there's a God.' Then you don't even need to preach the gospel for now they know there's a living God in heaven.

There is coming a time when fear grips planet earth and many will turn to other sources for guidance. False religions will offer a smorgasbord of alternative doctrines. Only those grounded in the Scriptures will be kept from error. Witchcraft, séances, tarot card, palm readers, those who practice astrology and spiritualist mediums will all pretend to have an answer as to why God is hiding His face. All of this has been expressly forbidden by the Lord (Lev.19:31; 20:2, Deut.18:11). Enthusiasm for fortune-tellers is proof that a people have withdrawn treacherously from God. We have been warned that doctrines of demons will be rampant in the last days (I Tim.4:1–7). Those with familiar spirits may chirp and sputter but the voice of the Lord when He speaks is like a trumpet that is clear and easily understood (Rev.4:1).

"Should not a people inquire of their God?" It is time for the church to cry out with night and day intercession. When God hides His face, we stir our hearts from the sanctuary to seek Him until we find Him. **"To the law and the testimony!"** The Word of God is a more sure source of wisdom. Every Word from God is pure and imparts life to those who receive it. May there be an army of bold ones who speak this out to all the new age insanity around us — **"To the law and the testimony!"**

"If they do not speak according to this word, they have no light of dawn." The light of dawn is the hope of Jesus Christ. Is the light of dawn growing inside of you? The path of the righteous is like the light of a sunrise shining in the eastern sky. From dark, to dim, to bright it increases. To forsake prayer and the Scriptures in a time of chaos is to reject our only true hope in the Son of God. In times of calamity, make sure you quiet your heart and seal up the Word of God in your soul. The dawning of Christ's glory is coming. For us, the early rays of morning light are shining.

So they go into exile, exasperation and despair. Without the hope of heaven and without any hope on earth — **"Distressed and hungry they will roam through the land."** Their difficulties will not bring them to faith and repentance, but to a hardening of heart that blinds them further. Cursing God becomes the venting of their bitter condition. "They will become enraged, and looking upward, will curse their King and their God." The true King of heaven and His claims will be rejected and cursed from their mouths. All the earth will know that Jesus is coming back as King but not all the earth will praise Him, some will curse instead.

"Darkness", **"gloom"**, and **"utter darkness."** Three different Hebrew words used to describe their deplorable condition. Instead of running to God in the light of His mercy and grace in His Sanctuary, they curse Him with increasing darkness surrounding their hearts. Divine justice has now given them what they loved — darkness! This is the fruit of abandoning God and refusing His Word as truth.

Isaiah is now ready to bring the revelation of the God born of a virgin, Immanuel. The 'God-with-us' Savior will be born and bring great light in the midst of this darkness and gloom. His kingdom and His peace will have no end.

Immanuel, we love you!

To be continued....

About the Author

Brian & Candace Simmons have been in active ministry for 30 years. They have served as tribal missionaries planting churches among the Kuna Indians, overseeing translation and consultant work. While in the jungle, they were visited by the Holy Spirit in a revival that brought many native people to salvation in Jesus Christ. This revival introduced the Simmons to the prophetic power of the end-time purposes of God. Brian has authored a number of books that focus on the purposes of God for this generation. They are convinced that God's Spirit will be poured out in revival power upon the nations of the earth, including the

United States and New England, before the return of our Lord Jesus.

The passion of their ministry has been to equip this generation to become radical lovers of Jesus Christ. Their joy is mentoring young people, helping many find their place of ministry in the Body of Christ. Stairway Ministries has been established for that purpose. Brian is also the Sr. Pastor of Gateway Christian Fellowship in West Haven, Connecticut where they make their home. They are blessed with three children and four grandchildren. For more information on Stairway Ministries and a complete listing of their teaching materials, contact:

Stairway Ministries
P.O. Box 26512
West Haven, CT 06516
203-934-0880
stairwayministries@hotmail.com

WHAT WAS IT LIKE FOR ADAM TO BE KISSED BY HIS CREATOR?

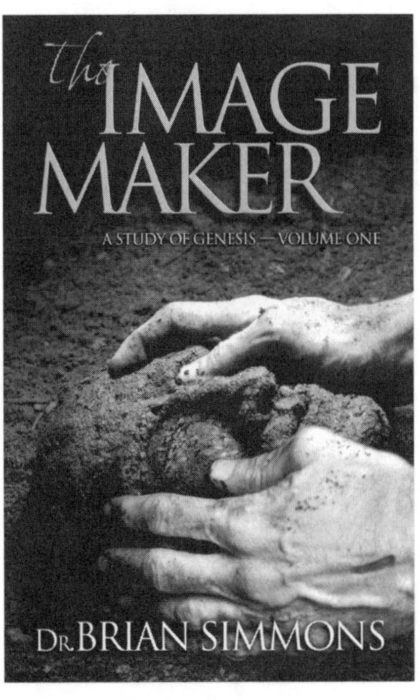

God is truly The Image-Maker who satisfied His voluntary loneliness by making you and I! In this fascinating study of the first chapters of Genesis, the author takes us deeper into the mysteries of the very moment Adam looked into the eyes of The Image-Maker. Weaving a story as he unfolds the Scriptures, Brian Simmons takes you closer to the One who stamped this Image upon your life. You are a carrier of His likeness! *The Image-Maker* is the first of three volumes that will unlock the book of Genesis to a new generation. Be prepared to gather new insights into the ancient message of Genesis as He touches you! The Image-Maker puts Himself into human vessels. And this is only the beginning!

To be continued....

THE STAIRWAY LEADS TO HEAVEN

It is the portal opened on earth that escorts God's people into the heavens. There is a stairway to heaven spoken of in the Bible and that Stairway is a Man, Jesus Christ. *"I tell you the truth, you shall see heaven open, and the angels of God ascending and descending on the Son of Man." John 1:51* The Jacob journey brings us all to this Stairway. Come and go up into a higher realm of seeing God's promises ready to be fulfilled. In this epic story of Abraham, Isaac, and Jacob you will see how God becomes real to His people. The way God leads Abraham into deeper faith, the way God leads Isaac to his bride, and the way God led Jacob to the Jabbok is exactly the way God leads you. Get ready to discover the Stairway into destiny, the journey of a lifetime.

ORDER FORM

➢ ORDER ONLINE: http://www.stairwayministries.org

➢ CALL TOLL-FREE (U.S. AND CANADA): 1-877-527-0880

➢ FAX ORDERS (U.S. AND CANADA): 1-203-937-6822

➢ POSTAL ORDERS: Stairway Ministries, P.O. Box 26512,
West Haven, CT 06516 USA

QUANTITY	TITLE	PRICE	TOTAL
________	SONG OF SONGS: THE JOURNEY OF THE BRIDE	$12.00	________
________	PRAYER PARTNERS WITH JESUS	$12.00	________
________	IMAGE MAKER	$12.00	________
________	THE STAIRWAY	$12.00	________
________	THE DREAMER	$12.00	________
________	ISAIAH: THE PROPHET OF ZION	$12.00	________
		SUBTOTAL	________
		SHIPPING (20% OF SUBTOTAL)	________
		TOTAL THIS ORDER	________

(PLEASE PRINT CLEARLY)

NAME:____

STREET ADDRESS: ________________________________

APT.____________________ CITY:____________________

STATE:____________________ ZIP:____________________

COUNTRY:__________________ PHONE:__________________

E-MAIL:____

METHOD OF PAYMENT:

___ Check or Money Order (Make check payable to Stairway Ministries)

___ Credit Card: ___ Visa ___ MasterCard ___ American Express ___ Discover

CARD NUMBER: _______-_______-_______-_______ EXPIRATION DATE: _____/______

CARD VALIDATION NUMBER: (last three digits on the back of your card) ___________

CARD HOLDER (please print): ________________________________

SIGNATURE:____

(Credit card orders cannot be processed without signature)

For current shipping and handling information, call 1-877-527-0880.
Or visit our web site at www.stairwayministries.org.